RANDOM THOUGHTS

August 2019

Dakota -

Wishing you
many random thoughts.

Anthony

RANDOM THOUGHTS

REFLECTIONS ON PUBLIC SERVICE, FATHERHOOD, AND MIDDLE AGE

ANTHONY J. ROMANELLO

To my all-season friend Diane, and our John, Domenic, Mary, and Anna who make "Romzoo" the best place in the world.

To Wendy Mallow, my right hand; Cathy Vollbrecht, *Random Thoughts* editor; and Jane Sutherland, *Random Thoughts* compiler.

To those who have encouraged me to extend the reach of *Random Thoughts* including my Dad and Uncle Mark.

To the elected officials who have given me the opportunity to serve.

And to Team Stafford, my colleagues in the calling to public service.

Thanks for all you do.

JANUARY 2008

THERE is a part of every January that I dislike. It's not the cold weather or trying to lose the holiday pounds I added. Every January, my daughter appears in the ballet *The Nutcracker*. As a loving, dutiful dad, I sit through more than two hours of production and smile, all the while questioning my manhood. It is an even greater insult that the recital is always scheduled during the NFL playoffs.

As the dedicated dads arrived at the recital this past Saturday night, each of us was checking the Patriots–Jaguar score on our blackberries and making the obligatory comments about how much we would rather light our hair on fire than watch the ballet. The lights dim, the music starts, and the dancers come out. Little girls in period costumes move nervously to Tchaikovsky's powerful score. The older girls dance more confidently. After my four-year-old appears and it is still early in the ballet, I started looking around the room to kill the time. I noticed that these same men who dreaded the event were staring intently at the wordless drama unfolding in front of them. Some were moving their index fingers as if to conduct Tchaikovsky. Others were mesmerized by the sparkling scenery. I found myself in awe of the synchronization of all the dancers who move as one to the music.

Is a prima ballerina any less agile or athletic than a star running back? Is there any less grace or art in her twirling effortlessly and him driving through the secondary for a thirty-yard touchdown run? Art and beauty is in the eye of beholder. I came to the ballet in dread and left inspired by the art.

Sometimes in life, I make assumptions that may cause me to miss the art or beauty of what is in front of me. Is there art in what sounds like a crazy idea to save the county money? That seemingly hair-brained approach we refuse to attempt may just be the grace we need to get us through our current challenges. Is there beauty in the ideas in that trade publication that I give only a passing glance?

Next January, I will see *The Nutcracker* again. And I may just look forward to it. Maybe.

Thanks for all you do.

FEBRUARY 2008

EARLY in the morning of January 20, Stafford's E-911 Center was relocated from the basement of the Courthouse to the Humphrey Building (Stafford County Public Safety Center).

A very complex technical event, the switchover occurred after months of planning and testing. That Sunday morning, dozens of county staff left their homes to come to work. There were no complaints, just hard-working people who came to do a job. While most of Stafford's citizens will never know of the job's success, few would be unaware had it failed.

The good people that made the 911 switchover happen exemplify our commitment to serve our community. And I know it is only one such example of the numerous quiet, invisible acts of service county staff regularly perform.

The switchover was executed flawlessly, and just before sunrise, the first call in the Humphrey Building was handled by dispatchers Kristy Mancil and Tammy Embrey.

Most of Stafford slept through this event. You could say it is one of our B-E-S-T-kept secrets.

Thanks for all you do.

MARCH 2008

LAST week, David Gayle, MC Moncure, Scott Mayausky, Chief Rob Brown, First Sergeant Brian Jacobs, Deputy Craig Cain, and I attended Chairman Schwartz's meeting with the Falls Run neighborhood. About 150 residents were there to ask questions of their supervisor and county staff.

All my fellow staff members in attendance did a great job handling questions from the audience. Commissioner of the Revenue Scott Mayausky was especially adept at pointing out to the citizens that it was not *his* reassessment, but *my* budget that would raise their taxes!

The hallmark of the night was an elderly gentleman who stood up to thank Chief Brown for opening the Berea Fire Station. In a choked-up voice, the gentleman noted that since Berea opened on February 1, he had called 911 three times, and Berea responded all three times within two minutes.

Surely the responding team from Berea deserves the credit for three rescues along with the sheriff's deputies and 911 operators who assisted on the calls. Sharing that credit are all of the staff who worked to open Berea: Public Services built it, Information Technology wired it, Human Resources staffed it, and Finance bought the fire truck and paid the bills.

I wish every county employee could have been there to hear this man thank Chief Brown. None of us serves the public alone. Together we are enriching lives throughout this community.

Thanks for all you do.

APRIL 2008

DURING the recent tough budget discussions, my mind turned often to my grandmother. As a child, I would visit her yearly in Greenwich, Connecticut. Grandma lived with my aunt and survived on her social security check. She and my grandfather raised my dad and his three siblings through the Depression. Never well off, they were fortunate since my grandfather was a truck driver for Borden Milk and always had work during the Depression.

Grandma didn't waste anything. Coffee grounds were used for a week. When she made ravioli, the leftover slivers of dough were cooked up as egg noodles. Even the smallest portion of uneaten bread was saved to feed the birds.

Each visit, she would take me on the city bus to Woolworth's to buy tube socks. In those days, tube socks were sold one pair at a time. The socks had yellow and blue bands on top and fully stretched would go from my toes to my knees. She made sure they were the right size for my foot by wrapping the sock around my fisted hand (try it, it works).

Grandma never had a driver's license and never owned a car. She paid 60 cents for each of us to ride the bus. She always let me pull the string to let the bus driver know it was our stop. I never needed the socks, but she liked to buy them for me. I think back now and realize she probably bought the socks simply because she could. As a homebound elderly widow, riding that bus was a big part of her personal dignity.

What a great memory every time I see a bus (and long tube socks). As I think about our current budget discussions, bad coffee and egg noodles don't sound half bad. Grandma made the most of what little she had. It's a lesson that will resonate with me for the rest of my life.

Thanks for all you do.

MAY 2008

IT was one of those spring nights where our family had more places to be than people to get there. Diane took all the kids to St. Clair Brooks Park for John's baseball game. I rushed from work to meet her there, so I could watch the game, and she could take Mary to church. Domenic and Anna stayed with me so they could play at the park during the baseball game.

John was starting pitcher for the Stafford Orioles with Michael Sterne (son of Kathy in the Circuit Court Clerk's Office) as his catcher. They won 5–2.

On this crisp spring night, Domenic and Anna roamed all around the park together. They spent most of their time on the twenty-foot high mound of dirt that has become a very cheap and popular element for children who visit the park.

Domenic gave his five-year-old sister a piggyback ride. He pushed her on the swing. She knew that the only reason she was not immediately at my side was because she was in the care of her older brother. Domenic is much more fun than Dad or any old baseball game. They played together for two and a half hours, laughing and smiling, and came home covered head to toe in Stafford County dirt.

Are these my children? Aren't these the same kids

who fight over the last chocolate Pop-Tart? Didn't they just try to hurt each other in a dispute over watching *Hannah Montana* vs. *Sponge Bob*? Diane and I are not at dinner to eat; we are there to referee!

At home, our kids often have to be separated. When we leave the house, they rarely are apart from each other. Families take care of each other.

My college roommate was traveling from DC recently and stopped in the office to meet me for lunch. He arrived early, so he sat outside the conference room waiting for my meeting to end. It was a lively discussion on the budget—laughter to be sure but also a healthy conflict of viewpoints among staff. My friend heard the whole discussion.

When we went to lunch, he said, "I want a job with Stafford County." For us, the meeting was a spirited, painful budget debate. For him, it was a group of people who enjoy each other and work really well together, laughing through the tough times.

Families take care of each other.

Thanks for all you do.

JUNE 2008

THE Sunday night before Memorial Day, my eight-year-old daughter Mary and her brother were wrestling on the floor. In the tussle, she slammed her head on the corner of my desk leaving a one-inch long gash in the back of her head that was pouring blood.

We all jumped in the car and headed to the Falmouth Fire Department, only a few hundred yards from our home. The good firefighters gave us a gauze pad and offered to call the ambulance. We decided we would take her to the Mary Washington ER ourselves.

We flew down Butler Road, waited an eternity at the Falmouth intersection, and then sped down Route 1. We barreled into the waiting room and headed to the check-in counter. The ER staff asked us to sit down and fill out several pages of paperwork.

Sit down?! My daughter's head is open, and you want me to sit down? I don't want to sit down. I want Marcus Welby, Dr. McDreamy, Hawkeye Pierce, anybody! And I want him now.

They gave us several forms to complete.

Fill out paperwork? My daughter's head is bleeding. I would have signed over the deed to my house. In the waiting room, Animal Planet's *Meerkat Manor* was on television. *How do they tell the meerkats apart? They all look alike.* The kids kept themselves occupied by a twenty questions

21

card game from Chik-Fil-A. *I don't care how you ask them. It just doesn't take twenty questions to guess the word "banana"!*

As it turns out, head gashes are not uncommon, so we waited to be seen. A young boy with a 105-degree fever arrived. A young man had some terrible cut on his leg, which his girlfriend had bandaged with a washcloth and masking tape. A poor young woman dressed to go dancing was doubled over with abdominal pain. An elderly woman complained of neck pain. Several other people sat quietly in their misery—all of us totally dependent on the good doctors and nurses at the ER and hoping our name would be next.

The ER staff understands priorities. That is their business. And while the gauze pad was soaked with blood, as we looked around the room, we came to realize there were others more in need than Mary.

Balance in life is all about setting priorities. For me, it is hands-down the hardest of the BEST values. The ER example was a good one for me. Maybe that work I take home is a cut finger, but reading *Curious George* is a 105-degree fever. Playing catch or dancing to *Rockstar* is a heart attack while responding to an afterhours e-mail is a sprained ankle. Next time I tell the kids I don't have time to play, I will think of that calm ER nurse who knew her priorities.

Our ER visit took three hours. One shot and six staples later, Mary Romanello is no worse for the experience. Her dad is still trying to figure out how to tell the meerkats apart.

Thanks for all you do.

JULY 2008

MY mother's parents lived on Third Street in New Rochelle, New York. Both came to America from Southern Italy. My grandfather was a landscaper, and they raised five children in a three-room duplex apartment.

When we would visit, lunch was served promptly at noon. Grandma would cook chicken cutlets. The chicken was cut wafer thin, breaded, and fried. It was served with pasta. The pasta was accented with just a little red sauce. We peppered the chicken and pasta with Parmesan cheese (served from a bowl with a spoon, not shaken from a green container with holes in the top as we do now). Salad was served with the meal (not before) and we ate it on the same plate as the chicken and pasta.

Grandma and Grandpa drank red wine from jelly glasses. We kids drank 7-Up from little glass bottles. For dessert, we had Grandma's biscotti—long wedge-shaped cookies enhanced by a generous amount of the liqueur anisette.

After lunch, we could play ball in the small concrete backyard or sit on the plastic-covered furniture in the living room to watch *All My Children* with Grandma. We always went outside. Grandpa would sit on the front porch watching the modest Third Street traffic.

With their thick Italian accents, my grandparents

couldn't pronounce the "th" in Anthony, so they called me *Antony*. When it was time to leave, we would kiss Grandpa on the cheek and then brace ourselves for Grandma's carwash kisses. Grandma would kiss me up one side of the face and down the other the whole time saying, "Antony, such a good boy, Antony."

The memory of Grandma and Grandpa helps me to remind myself that while life is rarely easy, it can often be simple.

The simplest efforts can add flavor and richness to our relationships with each other and citizens: a smile on a tough day, a thank you for a thankless job, a bag of M&Ms provided by a coworker to get you through the afternoon.

Grandma and Grandpa never had it easy, but they knew how to give life flavor. Whether it was their sweet Italian accents, anisette cookies, Parmesan sprinkled chicken, or carwash kisses, they gave richness and flavor to a simple life.

Thanks for all you do.

August 2008

WHAT is it about hair?

My preteen boys want their hair long. Not just long, but messy with scraggly strands covering their eyes. John's hair is so curly that when he was a toddler, strangers would tell me, "You have a beautiful daughter." Domenic's hair is straight as an arrow, and when it grows over his eyes, he looks like Cousin Itt.

I don't remember caring about my hair as a teenager (which may explain why I had so few dates). Where I wanted hair that would air dry in minutes, my boys want luscious locks.

We bought them gel and told them they could keep their hair long if it was neat, but the gel bottle was untouched, and the hair, burgeoned. I threatened them with a trip to the Quantico barbershop, and still the hair grew. This summer, I tried a different tactic. I told them that they could do whatever they wanted with their hair. But just before school starts in September, I would have their hair cut to my specifications.

My sister has adult children and tells me to pick my parenting battles by ignoring the hair. But how do I do that when my boys look like they should be on the cover of *Seventeen* magazine?

Pick your battles. How many times have I heard

that advice from family and colleagues? One of the most famous unnecessary battles was the Battle of New Orleans fought and won by General Andrew Jackson two weeks after the War of 1812 ended. The news of the peace did not reach Louisiana until after the battle. How many Battles of New Orleans have I fought? Of the battles that I may choose to fight, how many are really important and how many will be wasted energy?

Will my boys get pre-Labor Day buzz cuts? I am not sure. I have been distracted recently by another battle—my girls want their hair shorter.

Thanks for all you do.

September 2008

Do the bus, Dad.

JOHN, our oldest, started kindergarten in 2001. To prepare him to ride the school bus safely, I imitated the motion and sounds of a school bus. Since then, my annual first day of school imitation of a school bus has become a family ritual.

Anna started kindergarten this week, so it was another opportunity for me to do the bus. The middle school bus comes first, so we all waited out with John (now seventh grade), his brother, and the neighbor kids. Remembering how embarrassing my parents were to me at that age, I stood with him at the bus stop quietly. I figured "doing the bus" would be mortifying for him.

I have to admit embarrassing my kids is fun, but I do remember those painful teenage moments when my dad would say the wrong thing. He is a retired wastewater engineer, and when people would wince at his work-related stories, he noted, "We all contribute."

He loves to tell people how "little" Anthony (born 10 lbs. 4 oz.) needed one more bottle than all the other babies in the hospital nursery. And, of course, there were those many Saturdays when he would cut the grass with his shirt off . . .

So we were waiting for the middle school bus, and then John made my day. He said, "Dad, do the bus!"

I couldn't believe it! I paused for a moment and asked, "John, are you sure?"

He nodded, and a neighbor kid said, "Come on, we want to see it!"

So I did the bus. Never was a middle-aged man so happy to flail about in the street.

Too often I stop myself from doing something small to lift a friend's or colleague's spirits because I think, "That is just silly" or "You should do something really nice." But like John's simple request, light humor can often lift the spirit as much as heavy sentiment. I don't know if he will ask me to do the bus next year. I don't know why he would be embarrassed anyway; it's not as if his dad dresses in a chicken costume.

Thanks for all you do.

OCTOBER 2008

ANNA started kindergarten last month. On one of her first days in school, my wife packed her *High School Musical* lunch box with a bologna and cheese sandwich, raisins, bat-shaped Halloween pretzels, two cookies, and a juice box. Anna returned home that afternoon with an uneaten corner of her sandwich and the two cookies. A slow eater, Anna had run out of time to finish her sandwich and said, "Mommy, I am not allowed to have dessert without finishing my sandwich."

As soon as she said this, our three older kids immediately surrounded her and explained that she could have thrown away the sandwich, eaten the cookies, and Mom would have been none the wiser. While her parents were thrilled with her honesty, her siblings were disappointed by her lack of creativity.

Anna's honesty reminds me of the old saying "integrity is what you do when no one is watching." Stafford County is not perfect, but I can say in nearly five years here, I have rarely had to face an integrity issue. We are humans and do make mistakes, but generally, we are hardworking honest people who work every day to do right by the people of Stafford.

In a noisy cafeteria at Falmouth Elementary School,

a little girl remembered the rules and made her daddy proud.

I am going to eat all my vegetables tonight.

Thanks for all you do.

November 2008

THIS Tuesday, I played in the Department of Social Services Foster Care Tournament Fundraiser at Augustine Golf Club. The final score was,

Augustine 18
Romanello 0

It was my last game of golf. Not my last game this year—it was the last game of *my life*.

I am a bad golfer, a really bad golfer. With most sports, men are prone to exaggerate their accomplishments. We add fifty pounds to our highest bench press and describe minnows as marlins, but no man admits to being a good golfer. The truth is, however, my game is so bad that I would save time and money by simply walking the golf course and throwing balls into the woods and the ponds. One of my golf teachers, after many unsuccessful attempts to show me the finer points of the game, observed that watching me hold a golf club was like "eating sand."

After seventeen holes of the worst golf of my life, we were on the final hole of the tournament. My teammates had driven to the middle of the fairway ninety yards from the pin. I moved into position and announced to my teammates that this was the end of my golf career. While the pin was only ninety yards away, I pulled out my 8-iron and took two practice swings, both of which gently brushed the grass. I moved into position and took my final swing. The ball lifted high and stayed airborne for what seemed like five minutes before it landed softly on the green within ten feet of the hole. I strolled to the pin like Tiger headed to Augusta National's eighteenth green on Sunday afternoon.

But then this tournament was not really about me, or even golf. It was about some of Stafford's neediest kids. Many of these children take countless daily swings at affirmation or love but are shot down with negativity and hurt. It takes extraordinary effort to break a child's spirit but only simple, unconditional concern and attention to lift it. We may never know which hug, congratulations, or atta-boy or atta-girl sets a child on a course for a good future.

So I haven't put my golf clubs on eBay just yet. I may never be able to lift a golf ball, but I can certainly lift the spirit of a child.

Thanks for all you do.

DECEMBER 2008

WHAT is your favorite character from Charles Dickens's *A Christmas Carol*?

Is it Ebenezer Scrooge with his humbug attitude toward Christmas and cruel treatment of those around him? Is it the submissive Bob Cratchit or his feeble son, Tiny Tim, who in the end softens Scrooge's calloused heart? Is it one of the three ghosts who send Ebenezer down his path to reclamation? Is it the fair Belle, who, when Ebenezer turns her away to build his fortune, reminds us of opportunities lost? Is it Jacob Marley, cursed for eternity by the weight of his hardness?

My favorite is Fezziwig with whom the young Scrooge apprentices. In their look back into his early adult life, the Ghost of Christmas Past reminds Scrooge of the generous spirit of his first employer.

If there were a BEST values poster in nineteenth-century London, it would be on Fezziwig's warehouse wall. Christmas Eve comes, and Fezziwig directs that all work stop. He and his wife lay out a lavish spread of food. Musicians play, and the group dances late into the night. At the end of the night, Mr. and Mrs. Fezziwig greet each of their beloved staff and wish them the merriest of Christmases. Speaking to the Ghost of Christmas Past,

Ebenezer sums up Fezziwig's gift: "The happiness he gives is quite as great as if it cost a fortune."

Some organizational development consultant will likely create a Fezziwig-Scrooge Leadership Scale. Fezziwig loved life and the people around him; Scrooge's only love was his counting house, and he lived a miserable lonely existence. Both were successful businessmen, but one inspired while the other demoralized.

On any given day, I can be on either end of the Fezziwig-Scrooge scale, but in my annual read of *A Christmas Carol*, I am reminded that the promise of Dickens's message is that no matter where we fall today on that gauge, we can start a different course tomorrow.

Thanks for all you do. And may God bless us, every one.

JANUARY 2009

MY world is turning upside down. Our three older kids started their Christmas break with news about their "relationships."

John, thirteen, asked one of his classmates to be his girlfriend. She said yes. This is his second girlfriend since he started seventh grade.

Domenic, eleven, spent $11 of his own money on a heart locket necklace for his sixth-grade girlfriend. When he gave it to her, she couldn't work the clasp, so he had to hang it around her neck. My son can't keep his shoes tied or pull up his pants, but he can handle intricate jewelry?

Mary, nine, came home from school with a flower given to her by a boy in her class. My nine-year-old little girl has some boy after her! I immediately called Sheriff Jett to initiate an investigation into this third-grade troublemaker.

I am consoled by Anna, five, in whose world all problems can be solved with Band-Aids, hugs, or cookies. How satisfying it is for me when Anna comes just before bed, points to the tiny scratch on her foot, and requests a Band-Aid. Careful not to touch the sterile part, I seal the Band-Aid to her foot (assuming the foot was clean in the first place) and give her a kiss on the forehead. All is now well in her world. It is probably the only problem I have solved that day. For an injury with blood, she needs a long hug, and the worst offenses require an Oreo or Chips Ahoy to relieve the pain.

I wonder what life would be like if we all lived in Anna's world. What if a Band-Aid could be put on the budget book and our financial woes healed? Imagine a hug long enough that it not only attenuates but also removes the pain of life's suffering? Consider if an Oreo could be the pill for the diseases and cancers that affect our loved ones?

Are there enough Band-Aids for our financial statements? Should we begin staff meetings with a friendly embrace? What about Nutter Butters delivered to your desk every day at 2:00 p.m.? Surely, Band-Aids, hugs, and cookies are no permanent cure. But every Band-Aid, every hug, and every cookie has made me feel a little better and enabled me to look at the world in a slightly different light.

The investigation report just came in from the sheriff's office. Mary's suitor has a clean record. *I am watching you, little boy!*

Thanks for all you do.

FEBRUARY 2009

FEBRUARY turns my thinking to groundhogs.
While the groundhogs are still hibernating,
Groundhog Day reminds me of spring and summer
nights when the groundhogs stand on the side of the
road in the ravine across from the new Stafford hospital.
They are positioned on their hind legs with their front
legs pursed together like they are clapping. I am sure they
are applauding county employees returning home after
another day of service. I can hardly hear them, but I am
sure they are saying to each of us:

"Great job today, Stafford. See you tomorrow."

Groundhogs are consummate public servants. Their
tunnels begin downward, turn upward, and then go hori-
zontally to prevent flooding—a storm water solution
our Erosion and Sediment Control staff would surely
approve. Their tunnels have one primary entrance and
four exits, duly complying with the fire marshal's requirements for safe ingress/egress. Their lengthy tunnels are
less than 2,500 square feet of land disturbance to avoid
any permitting requirements (this is important since the
permit counter in Code Administration is too high for
groundhogs). Standing on the side of the road, groundhogs obey local traffic laws as opposed to possum, deer,
raccoons, and beavers who are still answering the question

why they (and the chicken) cross the road. And despite having three to five children annually, all groundhogs are home-schooled, saving Stafford County Public Schools millions annually.

The average groundhog lives six years in the wild. Imagine what the courthouse groundhogs have seen in their short life span. Are they excited about the new hospital, hoping there is a veterinarian on staff? When the HOT lanes are built on I-95, will they install signs on Route 1 directing commuters away from their earthen homes? What is their position on the proposed comprehensive plan for the county—would they add a dandelion overlay district for ample food supply?

Spring is coming. With spring, the courthouse groundhogs will awaken from their cold slumber and resume their roles of thanking us for serving their community. This April, on your way home, wave to our furry neighbors, take a bow, and listen closely to them say,

"Great job today, Stafford. See you tomorrow."

Thanks for all you do.

APRIL 2009

I will never forget little Jonelle.

My first full-time job in local government began this day seventeen years ago—April 6, 1992. I was one of nineteen newly hired benefits programs specialists in the City of Richmond's Department of Social Services. Our job was to screen families for food stamps and Aid to Dependent Children (now called TANF) where eligible families receive monthly financial support. We had three days to process food stamp applications for homeless people, thirty days for regular food stamps, and forty-five days for financial assistance.

The ink barely dry on my college diploma, I prided myself in ensuring that applicants received their benefits as soon as possible. My efficiency and accuracy numbers were high. On our "intake days," we would see fifteen to twenty clients in quick interviews for initial screening.

One intake day, Jonelle and her mom came to my interview desk. Recently homeless, they received an expedited review, so I said to them, "You will have your food stamps today."

Upon hearing this, Jonelle's face lit up. She threw her arms into the air and yelled, "Yeah, Mommy, we get to eat!"

I froze. Little Jonelle turned me into Jell-O. I had

already processed dozens of cases in my new job, but for the first time, it was real to me that Jonelle and her mom were not just a case number. I had efficiency and accuracy statistics for my caseloads, but no figures on making a difference in the lives of families. I could open those musty brown case folders and crank numbers with the best of them, but I soon realized that inside those folders was a complex story of personal suffering and pain.

I wish I could tell you that little Jonelle made me a better caseworker, but I don't have that wonderful gift that enables human services professionals to help families turn their lives around, often in the midst of incomparable adversity. Jonelle is with me, however, in all my considerations, and I hope the memory of her hopeful little face makes me a better public servant.

Jonelle is twenty-one years old now, the same age I was when I handled her mom's food stamp case. While you won't find Jonelle's food stamps on my résumé, I do count it as one of the accomplishments of my career—I helped a little girl.

Often, the lasting accomplishments in local government, as in life, are unseen.

Thanks for all you do.

MAY 2009

BORN May 1, 1909, Nanny would have been one hundred years old today.

She was my "third" grandmother, the mother of my stepmom, and I knew her only for the last twenty-three years of her life. We lost her in 2007.

She was born six years after the Wright Brothers and left this world just before Twitter. A lifelong Richmond resident, she would tell us about riding a horse and buggy with her sister from Richmond's Church Hill neighborhood to Goochland County to visit relatives. The trip was about thirty miles and took all day.

It was no mistake that her birthday was the first of May. In the old traveling circus, a "First of May" was the term for a first year performer. Throughout her long life, Nanny never lost her naïve and optimistic outlook. She loved to laugh and could find the silver lining on any cloud. A tiny woman, she was barely five feet tall and ate very little real food. But after a bird-size dinner, she could easily consume three scoops of ice cream—any flavor. She loved green and red Chuckles candies and kept a candy jar piled high with them on her coffee table.

What did I learn from Nanny? Was it some transcendental philosophy only the learned can appreciate? No, it was three basic life lessons.

Take genuine interest in each other. She never met a stranger. She could get anyone to talk. After meeting Nanny, mimes have been forced to end their careers. It would take her only a few minutes to know your family background, career experience, and shoe size. Her techniques were recently adopted by the FBI.

Love your family. She loved her family. She beamed with pride every time she mentioned a child, grandchild, or relative. She knew intimate details of each of our lives and took pride in tracking birthdays of many dozens of special people.

The greatest lesson—life is rarely easy, but it can often be simple. She weathered many ups and downs in her ninety-seven years with a smiling face, an open heart, and lots and lots of ice cream.

I think her three life lessons would fit into one Twitter message.

Thanks for all you do.

JUNE 2009

MARY'S third-grade class wrote essays on what they would do if elected president. Mary's list included the following:

- No killing.
- No being mean.
- No peas or green beans.
- A school day with two hours of recess, twenty minutes of math, and free lunches.
- A mall where everything is $10.
- Living in the largest house in the world with maids that follow all her direction.

I laughed when I read that in Mary's world green vegetables are equally offensive as taking another person's life. And I was inspired by her child-like faith that one woman can change the world. Why not dream big?

After all, Martin Luther King Jr. didn't stand at the Washington Mall to tell America he had a four-point plan. He had a dream. Lincoln didn't sheepishly free slaves with a memorandum. He proclaimed their emancipation for all the world to see. Mother Teresa started with a small ministry and dedicated her life to reduce suffering for millions. And Mary Romanello dreams of a world where people are not hurt by violence, hatred, or green vegetables.

While few may change *the* world, I am convinced that everyone can change *a* world. In our daily encounters, we have the gift of being able to change *a* world for someone in need.

Mary has twenty-six years before she is old enough to be president. Until then, we all have to finish our green beans.

Thanks for all you do.

JULY 2009

I have a new life's goal.

My new life's goal is to be the man that my young children think I am.

In reading my kids' schoolwork from the past year, there are references to me as the world's smartest, funniest, and most handsome dad (all four kids are receiving eye exams this summer).

I remember well how I idolized my father from early childhood until I was about thirteen. Then at age thirteen, I had the epiphany that he is an imperfect man. And from the time I was thirteen until about twenty-two, his imperfections increased as I advanced through my teenage years.

Born in 1928, my dad carried the torch with President Kennedy as the "new generation of Americans—born in this century, tempered by war, disciplined by a hard and bitter peace." A child of the Depression, he was a minor league ballplayer, a two-time Korean War veteran, and a widower who raised five kids. He finished his engineering degree in two and a half years on the GI Bill. At age eighty, he and my stepmother serve as Henrico County election officials, and he is president of his HOA. He still laments the baseball Giants leaving New York. His voice won't get him on *American Idol*, but his Lindy may be good enough for *Dancing with the Stars*.

My dad is neither the perfect man I believed him to be when I was nine nor is he the wholly imperfect soul I believed him to be when I was seventeen. What is most admirable about my father is what he accomplished in light of his human flaws. What we do with our strengths is less remarkable than how we live in spite of our weaknesses.

Over the next few years, all four of my children will be teenagers, so I know my days as the world's "most awesome" dad are numbered.

I do hope that when I collect Social Security, my children will observe, "Dad is not perfect, but he did okay."

Thanks for all you do.

AUGUST 2009

I miss being bored.

I don't mean sitting in a long meeting bored. I mean the summer boredom of a child—day after day of fun and freedom linked together by hours of boredom. How I wish I could return to that boredom!

When I was nine to thirteen years old, my family lived in Huntington Beach, California, on the Pacific coast. Summer days were positively perfect (imagine Virginia in late June with no humidity). My friends Glenn, Eric, David, and I would spend most of the daylight hours together. Three days a week, Glenn's mom would load us into her Corvair van and take us to the beach for the day. No suntan lotion necessary, just a Boogie board, towel, and a bologna and ketchup sandwich for lunch.

On the nonbeach days, we would troll the neighborhoods on our bikes. We would head to the Thrifty drug store for a thirty-five-cent double cone. On Tuesdays, we would go to Der Wienerschnitzel for the ninety-nine-cent lunch special: hot dog, small fries, and a small Coke. (We'd order two specials each).

David had a tandem Schwinn which one of us would ride around hoping the neighborhood girls would ask for a ride. Once Staci, Tina, or Mandy were sitting in the back seat, we would drive her through the neighborhood at a crazy speed, finding every tight turn and bump in the road. When the ride ended, our damsel in distress would usually smack us in the face, but the laughs were worth it.

On the rare rainy day, we played Atari or Intellivision. Or we were driven to the movies and dropped off for the day. In a midlife confession, I admit we would pay for one movie, head to the bathroom after the movie, and then into another theater. How our parents never figured out that one movie is not eight hours long is beyond me! We did pay for Jujyfruits.

And in between the movies, the beach, the bikes, and scaring the neighborhood girls, there were hundreds of hours of boredom each summer. How I miss that. In our very busy, hectic world, there is very little chance for boredom. Sometimes when rushing from place to place, I think a little boredom might be a good thing.

As kids do, my kids complain about being bored. When they do, I smile to myself and think of that tandem Schwinn.

Thanks for all you do.

September 2009

EARLY in my career, I was dispatched with seven of my colleagues to Lawton, Oklahoma, to preview software we were considering purchasing. An otherwise sleepy town, Lawton is dominated by the presence of Fort Sill, the army's field artillery school.

To head home, we were catching a 6:00 a.m. puddle jumper out of the Lawton airport to a connecting flight at Chicago O'Hare. As this was the prehomeland security days, we arrived at the airport a little over an hour before our flight. When we arrived, the airport was still closed for the night.

Just before 5:00 a.m., an airport employee walks up, unlocks the doors to the airport, and lets us in. We head to the ticket counter, and the same lady is there to check us in. She is careful to point out that our flight is leaving from Gate 1, even though both gates leave from the same terminal. We sit around talking while waiting to board and then hear a familiar voice. There she is again in the terminal. Even though the eight of us are the only ones in the airport, she calls our boarding *by row*. As we head out to the plane, there she is again loading our luggage! (She was not the pilot.)

If you asked the Lawton Airport employee to describe

her job, she would likely say, "To help people get where they want to go."

Is our job any different?

Thanks for all you do.

OCTOBER 2009

MY favorite book was written in 1970. It has twenty-six pages and full-color illustrations.

Surely, I love Steinbeck and O. Henry. I read all of David McCullough's histories and Dan Brown's thrillers. But my favorite book of all time stands out not for its contribution to the literary world, but for its memories. It is the Berenstain Bears's *Old Hat New Hat*.

Since my oldest child could sit in my lap, I have enjoyed reading it to my kids. The story is simple. A bear decides his torn, patched hat needs to be replaced. He tries on dozens of hats including a series described as "too beady," "too bumpy," "too leafy," "too lumpy," "too twisty," "too twirly," "too wrinkly," "too curly." In the end, he is unimpressed with the fancy hats and realizes his old hat is "just right." The bear leaves the hat shop with a wide grin as the hat store clerk glares at him for making him work so hard.

We have read the book so many times, its broken spine is held together by clear packing tape.

Recently, I volunteered to read to Anna's first-grade class. I selected my all-time favorite, but she said no. Anna decided that the must-read selections would be the recent classics *Pinkalicious* and *Purplicious*. My favorite book was kicked to the curb. I suppose the Berenstain Bears are a little pedestrian for first-graders.

The days of my kids climbing into my lap and listening to me read *Old Hat New Hat* are over. How I will miss those days. Just like the bear's old hat, that torn tape-sewn book is one my life simple joys, but now it is relegated to the dusty shelves with the long unread *Goodnight Moon*, *Green Eggs & Ham*, and *The Cat in the Hat*. Childhood has as many rites of passage for the parent as for the child.

So if anyone is interested, I will read *Old Hat New Hat* to you. Anybody?

If you let me, I'll be your best friend.

Thanks for all you do.

November 2009

THANKSGIVING is a time to count blessings. There is no greater blessing in this world than the people with whom we share it. Among my many blessings, I am thankful for the following:

- *Derrick Carr* whose grueling daily run shames me into getting on the treadmill.
- *Kari Matheny* and *Camilla Shover* who keep the pools going swimmingly even when the rip tides rage.
- *Gerald "Jazz" Jaskulski* whose weather reports keep me in the know.
- *Cathy Riddle* and *Michele Lansford* whose weekly 'Cooler fills us with hope.
- *Jeff Shover* who could make the Grim Reaper laugh.
- *Jeff Harvey and the Planning staff* who keep smiling through *every* comprehensive plan revision.
- *Steve Carey* whose unmarked police cruiser is more for spreading hope than locking up bad guys.
- *Rachel Hudson* who makes unpopular decisions with such grace.
- *Andrew Mikel and the Landfill staff* who take every man's trash and make our landfill an environmental treasure.

- *Joe Howard* whose dry sense of humor enlivens board meetings.
- *The Utilities Field Operations Crews* who always go with the flow, day or night.
- *David Noel and the IT staff* who keep us all connected.
- *Matt Warren* who blocked Warrenton Road until I emptied my wallet for Jerry's Kids.
- *Laura Rudy* who is a first-class act in six million ways.
- *DeVonne Johnson* whose golf tips keep others safe while I'm swinging.
- *Donna Krauss and Sue Clark (Schools)* whose autism program helps children with disabilities become adults with possibilities.
- *Judy Barnes* who did sell ice to Eskimos to raise funds for United Way.
- *MC Moncure* who reminds us that Stafford's past is also her future.
- *Barbara Decatur, Nicole McGuire, Jim Thompson, and their staff* who administer a gallon of justice in a quart jar.
- *The Social Services Staff* who, in addition to their "day jobs," will see that three thousand Stafford families have Thanksgiving dinner.
- *Wendy Mallow* who works closer to me than anyone and yet still manages to keep her sanity.

- *The Board of Supervisors* who give me a chance to make a difference.
- *All my fellow employees* whose daily miracles make Stafford home for 30,000 families and 2,500 businesses.

Best wishes to all for a happy, safe, and restful Thanksgiving.

Thanks for all you do.

DECEMBER 2009

DID you remember to kiss your wife today?
One morning when I was town manager in West
Point, I was rushing out the door to work. I gave each
of my kids a kiss on the head and left. I was headed
down the driveway to my car when Diane said, "Hey,
what about me?" I forgot to kiss my wife good-bye!

Later that day in West Point, I told my coworkers that
I forgot to kiss Diane. When I left the office that night,
there was a sticker on the steering wheel of my car that
read, "Did you remember to kiss your wife today?" My
work family helped me take care of my home family. I
never forgot again.

Local government is a family affair—an experience
not just for us employees but also for our spouses and
children. While we all strive for work-life balance, the
demands of public service can cause us to miss family
events, baseball games, dance recitals, and awards assem-
blies. And since we serve the public every day, many of
our colleagues work Sundays, holidays, and nights when
other moms and dads are with their children.

The 2008 Tornado struck the Thursday before
Mother's Day. After three long days of work, I told all
of the mothers to stay home and rest that Mother's Day.
None of them listened to me. They all came in to help

the families of England Run North—and made sure their children had flowers to give to their moms on Mother's Day.

Staffing levels and budgets are only part of what we need to serve the public. The other critical ingredient is loving and supportive families. Indeed, as our budgets get smaller and our responsibilities greater, it is our families that will sustain us.

Did you remember to kiss your wife today?

The little sticker on my car in West Point was greater than any present I ever found under the Christmas tree. It was a daily reminder of who makes it possible for me to serve others.

Merry Christmas.

Thanks for all you do.

And to our families—thanks for all *they* do.

JANUARY 2010

HAITI.
Seismologists will debate how.

Theologians will question why.

I have neither the intellect nor the depth of understanding to answer why or how; I just want to help.

My mind and desk in Stafford are full of work to be done, but my heart is in Port-Au-Prince, wishing I could be there pulling lost souls out of the rubble, washing the faces of bloody, dust-covered children, and sharing the inconsolable grief of the survivors. I have never been to Haiti, but today, I feel as if the island is my home.

While I did not feel those terrible tremors, I do feel the aftershock. Every CNN video, every newspaper photograph, every e-mail update shakes me up. I will pray, but I want to *do*. I want to comfort and serve. I ache to help. I share their pain.

Human tragedies are suffered by those who experience them and shared by all who know about them. We help both to serve others and to console ourselves.

It is not for me to understand how the plates beneath the earth shifted to cause this horrific storm. And why thousands perished is a question for the ages. How or why the Haiti earthquake happened matters little to me.

I just want to help.
Thanks for all you do.

FEBRUARY 2010

FIFTY men and boys set out for a sixteen-hour cruise. Saturday night, Domenic's Scout Troop boarded the USS *Constellation* in Baltimore's Inner Harbor for a real-life nineteenth-century tall ship experience. In the February cold and wind, the boys were dubbed "ship's boys" and told they would wait at least two hours for dinner while they learned the workings of the sails. As I stood there and froze, I could see people streaming into the Renaissance Hotel enjoying their $300 per night suites.

When dinner came, we were served beef stew, vegetable soup, dried fruit, hard tack, and lemon water. Hard tack was a first for many of us. Imagine a large, rock-hard flavorless saltine. The hard tack's flavor was diminished by my view of the Cheesecake Factory and P.F. Changs, only a stone's throw away from my nineteenth-century temporary prison.

After dinner, we toured the four-deck unheated boat. The captain's quarters were sumptuous and contained the only privy on the boat. Our sleeping quarters was one large room with hammocks. Light's out was 10:00 p.m. Before climbing into our hammocks, fifty men and boys removed their shoes. That began a night filled with the sounds and smells of fifty males. While hammocks worked well for the Skipper and Gilligan, they don't work for me. I lay still on my back, knowing that if I were to try to roll over onto my side, I would land on the kid next to me. The brightly lit Hyatt Hotel over the starboard side beckoned.

Two adults and two kids had to perform an hour of "night watch." This was a fire watch to satisfy the City of Baltimore's fire codes and also to ensure that no stray Scout found himself swimming in the night. During our hour, Domenic and I and our team patrolled all decks with quiet rigor. We acted like *CSI*, but our night watch was probably more *Mall Cop*. The night watchmen were required to ring the ship's bell every thirty minutes. As we lay in the hammocks, the oft-ringing bell reminded us of too little sleep and too much odor.

Reveille was 6:00 a.m. Breakfast was instant oatmeal, one piece of bacon, and a roll. The boys learned how to shoot cannons and then were given their "ship's boy" approval by the master at arms.

It was 30 degrees that night, and the February wind went right through my long johns. With Ruth's Chris Steak House and Vaccaro's Bakery in sight, we ate hard tack. With the Hotel Intercontinental calling, we slept in cold, crowded hammocks. When Diane asked me about the trip Sunday afternoon, I said with complete sincerity, "It was great."

The *Constellation* experience reminded me of our own work in responding to the blizzards of 2009 and 2010. Sure, other localities have bigger budgets, more staff, and fancier equipment. Our storm response combines the best efforts of our people, our resources, and our amazing volunteers to serve the public. Like the 2008 tornado, county staff tirelessly served our community with distinction.

Stafford's *Constellation* can outrun any other locality's modern-day destroyer. *Other localities may have more people and stuff, but nobody has more hustle than Stafford.*

I will visit the *Constellation* again. But I will be viewing the great ship from the picture window at the Cheesecake Factory.

Thanks for all you do.

MARCH 2010

ANGELA Matson left us last week. In her seventeen-month battle, cancer took her health but not her spirit.

She left behind two sons, a granddaughter, her parents, family, and many, many friends.

Angela's co-worker Lynn Clements remembered her friend:

We have had the pleasure of working with Angela, both in Finance and in the Utilities Department. She was a remarkable person—a good friend and a tremendously gifted people-person. We were amazed at the ease with which she could meet new people and instantly, they would take a liking to her. Her laughter and personality just bubbled over . . . it was contagious . . . it would make everyone around her feel better. We knew that we could count on her—and laugh with her—and cry with her. She loved us for who we are. If she noticed our faults, she ignored them—or laughed with us about them. She always made us feel good—even while she was not feeling good. Her outlook was nothing short of inspiring—always positive, always caring for others and always trusting in God's plan. We learned so much from her and we know that we have been truly blessed that our lives have crossed paths with hers.

To her family, and especially her sons Joe and Jeremy, we just want you to know how much we loved Angela and we thank you for sharing her with us.

Angela insisted on coming in to work every day her frail body would allow. With an ever-present smile on her face, her suffering was hard to see.

For those of us lucky enough to have known her, her hope lives on.

Angela, thanks for all you do.

MAY 2010

THIS year I will turn forty years old. Reaching middle age is a time for me to reflect on the following:

- My age has finally caught up with my waistline.
- My hair is no longer "prematurely" gray.
- Music seems louder now.
- My kids think Bon Jovi is classic rock.
- My seven-year-old can't understand why the DVR won't fast forward live television.
- When the neighborhood kids say "Mr. Romanello," I look around for my father.
- I mention Ralph Malph to younger county employees who think he's a Dr. Seuss character.
- A half-pint of milk in my elementary school cafeteria was 8 cents.
- I remember when the "stewardess" gave you a deck of cards when boarding the plane.
- Extreme temperatures bother me a lot more now.
- Muscles I didn't know I had hurt.
- I can nap anywhere. Anytime.

Middle age is like a fourth state of matter—I am neither young nor old.

- I stand a great distance from both my AARP membership and my kids' hip behavior.
- I am old enough to wear over-the-calf socks but too young to wear socks with sandals.
- I am young enough to not know the world without television but old enough to have lived when Watergate was just a salad.
- I am younger than the president, but I remember buying *Thriller* on vinyl.
- I wrote my high school assignments on an electric typewriter, but I can text on my Blackberry as fast as any teenager.
- And when I drink caffeine-free, calorie-free, sugar-free Diet Coke from an aluminum can, I try to imagine savoring Coca-Cola from a 12 oz. glass bottle.

So while I am not sure whether I am young or old, I do realize that middle age is a great gift.

The middle-aged George Bailey received the gift when Clarence the Angel showed him that his unrequited dreams didn't keep him from being the "richest man" in Bedford Falls. Three ghosts brought the gift to the middle-aged Ebenezer Scrooge that no regret is beyond reclamation when a generous heart is put to the task.

Now that I have traveled half of life's journey, I look down the road ahead and periodically glance in the rearview mirror. The mirror reflects life's triumphs and failures. I see the sufferings and joys of experience. I see the scar of regret and the blessings of good fortune.

The great gift of middle age is that this is the one point in my life, God willing, when the days ahead of me equal the days behind me.

No explaining ghosts haunt my sleep, and Clarence the Angel has yet to come my way. But I am grateful for the gift of middle age.

All this reflection has me tired; I think I need a nap.

Thanks for all you do.

JUNE 2010

MY son Domenic loves to go fishing. Since I am not much of a fisherman, when the opportunity came to go fishing the Rappahannock with a family friend who is an expert fisherman, we couldn't pass it up. Catfish were our quest.

Prior to heading out, I needed to buy a fishing license. I assumed there is *one* fishing license. Wrong. When I went to the state website, I found dozens of choices for different species of fish, times of the year, and types of water. After careful deliberation, I selected a freshwater permit for right-handed people of Italian descent fishing on a Friday afternoon. I paid my $16, and I was legal.

On the way to the river, I stopped to buy night crawlers. The worms were in the refrigerator on the same shelf with the milk products. The store had only Canadian night crawlers. I wondered if I was paying more for imported worms. I expected Canadian worms to be very polite and let out only a little "Ehh" when impaled on the hook.

The Rappahannock was calm, and our expert friend motored us to the perfect spot for catfish—along the riverbank just under trees that overhang the water. No sooner had the worms gone airborne then we had a bite. I am completely inept at fishing, but once that bobber went underwater, I imagined myself as Jacques Cousteau pulling in an eight-hundred-pound marlin. So what if it's just a two-pound catfish, I was experiencing the thrill of the hunt.

We caught eight catfish before the sky threatened a summer storm. Catfish live out of water longer than most fish, so when it was time to clean them, they were quite alive. Our expert fisherman employed a very humane method to send them to catfish heaven.

After this, the fish were filleted. We had sixteen beautiful catfish fillets, and so nothing was wasted, the fish carcasses were placed in the woods to feed the raccoons.

A few days later, I doused the fish in House Autry breading and put oil in the frying pan. Never having fried fish before, it seemed logical to me to put the stovetop at its highest setting. I let the oil get good and hot. I took two fillets and plopped them into the frying pan. As the fish landed, oil shot up and landed on my arm. I had small second-degree burns. I remembered as a child when I grabbed a handful of lit sparklers and burned my hand. My parents gave me a stick of butter to heal the burn. Today, we know it's better to cool a burn with water than to use butter to sauté our flesh.

Once in that hot oil, the fish immediately turned black and smoke filled the kitchen. I removed the pan from the stove, but the oil was too hot. It just wouldn't stop cooking. As the smoke filled other rooms of the house, it was like the fish were getting back me. We opened every window in the house and turned on every fan. The house smelled like charred fish for days.

I started with a new frying pan and heated the oil to a medium heat. The remaining fillets cooked to a golden brown delicious. I sampled the cooking with a guilty heart. My burnt arm ached. Before this experience, I never considered fried catfish a guilty pleasure. Eight catfish and numerous Canadian worms were expended for this quest. I love meat and fish, but I haven't had to spend a lot of time figuring out how they go from live animal to my dinner plate.

Like the fisherman who brings seafood from the river to our dinner table, the great effort and care in performing our work of public service is often invisible. Fishing for a good community is hard work.

My arm still hurts today. The catfish have the last laugh.

Thanks for all you do.

July 2010

STAFFORD Boy Scout Troop 516 just returned from a week at summer camp at Henderson Scout Reservation in rural Maryland, New York. My son Domenic and I joined thirty boys and twelve dads in the Catskill Mountains about twenty miles from Cooperstown, New York.

Our accommodations were canvas tents on wooden platforms, each with a metal bed frame and mattress. The canvas was aged and holey with duct tape and tarps applied to keep the rain out. The latrine was a two-holer with an odor as big and bold as the mountains around us. Throughout the camp was the Henderson mascot, chunky chipmunks who feasted on food and candy scraps left by Scouts.

For our first dinner, we cooked ground beef in a Dutch oven. We scooped the cooked beef into a Ziploc bag and added Fritos, lettuce, tomato, and cheese to make a Walking Taco. After dinner, we sat around the campfire, and the clear sky gave way to about six hours of powerful rain, thunder, lightning, and hail. At 1:00 a.m. in the midst of the torrents, I heard a siren in the distance. It blew for a couple of minutes. Thinking it might be an old-fashioned tornado warning, as a local government official, I felt compelled to find out what it meant. I called 911, and the very kind operator explained to me that is how they get the firefighters to respond.

How they get the firefighters to respond? Are you kidding me?
It's 2010. Haven't you heard of cell phones or radios?

We woke up at 7:00 a.m. that morning and breakfast was Mountain Man—a combination of sausage, eggs, hash browns, and cheese served in a soft tortilla. After breakfast, I headed down the path to find the showers.

There were six adult showers with wooden walls separating each shower. When I entered the showers, I was the only one there. Soon I heard someone come in to the next stall, and then I heard a voice—a *female* voice. She said, "Hi, how are you?"

I was frozen. I didn't notice that the showers were coed and did not expect to have a woman in the next shower. Finally, I composed myself and said, "Fine. How are you?" She kept talking and talking until I realized that she was talking on her cell phone. *I'm talking with a woman in a shower who isn't even talking to me.* I lathered and rinsed without repeating and bounded out of the showers.

After the Mountain Man and Walking Tacos, we shared all other meals with the other troops in the Henderson dining hall. The food was surprisingly good and plentiful. For lunch and dinner, there was peanut butter and jelly for those who couldn't handle the main course. In our health conscious new world, there was no "bug juice" served as it was when I was a boy, only milk and water. After every meal, we sang a song. On the first day, I didn't sing.

This is really stupid. I am not singing with two hundred kids.

By the second day, however, I couldn't wait for the song at the end of each meal. We sang songs in rounds and competed table to table to see who was the loudest.

After a couple of days, the regimentation of Scout Camp became comfortable and fun.

Every meal was served at a set time. Each table had a boy assigned to KP who followed a time-honored process for serving and cleaning up after each meal. The boys had three merit badge sessions daily and a little free time before and after dinner. We raised the flag quickly at sunrise and lowered it slowly at dusk. Taps was attempted nightly at 9:30 by a bugler with more tenacity than talent.

By Thursday, I was really missing my family and flush toilets. I drove in to Cooperstown.

The primary purpose of my trip was to use a real bathroom, but I masked my clandestine mission with a slice of Sicilian pizza and a cream soda from Joe's pizzeria. Later in the day, a basket of onion rings provided the same opportunity at the Double Play Cafe.

When you live in the woods, it doesn't take long to determine the true essentials of life.

Summer camp is a simple recipe of canvas tents,

peanut butter and jelly sandwiches, and good people. Indeed, with its foul latrines, holey tents, and portly chipmunks, the only elegant thing about Camp Henderson is its simplicity.

As we weather this Great Recession, we have certainly had to focus back to basics for our community. I wonder how we would approach our work if meetings were held not in conference rooms but in canvas tents with chipmunks at our feet. How would our decisions be enhanced if we sang songs at every staff gathering? Camp was a good reminder that while life is rarely easy, it can often be simple.

So I left camp with two goals: simplify my life and shower alone.

Thanks for all you do.

AUGUST 2010

THE man who hit baseball's "shot heard around the world" passed away earlier this month. In 1951, Bobby Thomson hit a ninth-inning three-run homerun in the final game of the National League pennant playoff series defeating the Brooklyn Dodgers and sending his New York Giants to the World Series.

Growing up in New York, my dad was a Giants fan; so when I heard of Bobby Thomson's death, my first thought was to talk with my dad. I asked him a simple question: "Dad, where were you that day?" This is what he told me . . .

In 1951, my dad was stationed on Japan's Kyushu Island serving in the army during the Korean War. There were two ways to keep in touch with stateside news during the Korean War—short wave radio and the weekly *Stars and Stripes* newspaper. Depending on where you were on the island, you might not have been to maintain a radio signal. With sketchy radio transmissions and a weekly newspaper, soldiers were always playing catch up on news other than the war situation. On Kyushu, the favorite radio program was the *Kyushu Kowboy*, which played daily at noon. (I remember watching *Hee Haw* with my dad in the 1970s, so I can assume from my dad's description, this was *Hee Haw* for radio.)

For the final game of the pennant playoffs, my dad was listening with Lt. Col. James W. Gerard on short wave radio. Lieutenant Colonel Gerard was what they called a $1 per year man. He took no military salary. His family lived in the affluent Manhattan suburb of Bronxville, New York, and owned property on Wall Street.

In the seventh inning, the radio went dead, and they missed the rest of the game. My dad, Lieutenant Colonel Gerard and all the army men of Kyushu Island didn't know the final score or hear about the "shot heard around the world" until two days later!

I knew my dad was serving in Japan in 1951, but I didn't know anything of the richness of his experience. One question brought the gift of a detailed reminiscence.

We spend a lot of time looking for answers. I wonder how our world would change if we simply asked good questions. A friend once gave me this advice: *take some time with a colleague, ask him one good question, and then shut my mouth.* Just listen, learn, and ponder the insight that the question brings. Questions are powerful. A good question followed by the asker's silence can provide a rich experience.

I will try to ask more questions. I wonder if *Hee Haw* is available on DVD.

Thanks for all you do.

September 2010

WHEN I call 411, the computer voice asks, "What city, please?" I just hate those computer voices and do what I can to confuse them. I try my best Nordic accent and say "Reykjavik, Iceland." Sometimes, I try a Jackie Gleason "homina, homina, homina." The computer immediately transfers me to a fellow human being.

When I am the only one in the fast-food restaurant and my order comes up, why do they announce on the microphone, "Number 875, your order is ready."

When I am lost in that big box retailer and finally track down a vested employee for help, their response is usually, "That is not my department, but I think what you're looking for is on the bottom shelf in aisle 76B." They then hand me MapQuest directions to find my way in the store.

Extraordinary customer service is more an aberration today than the normal. Some recent aberrations really made me think.

Traveling in Schenevus, New York, I stopped in the Chief Schenevus café for a midmorning snack. I was the only customer. The waitress brought me coffee and a piece of carrot cake. After she served me, she pulled the daily specials chalkboard off the wall and erased it. She drew that day's specials with slow painstaking effort.

Vivid colors were used to attract the eye. It would all be erased tomorrow morning, but today, it was her Mona Lisa.

In Georgetown one day, I stopped at a shoeshine stand to bring my dusty brown loafers back to life. The shoeshine artist was aged and bent over. A stained toothbrush cleaned the sole, new polish was applied, the shoes were rubbed with a cloth, and then finished with a brush. He worked for ten minutes as if I were a king having his shoes shined for a coronation. When he was finished, I paid his $5 fee and a tip. I wondered if I insulted him with a tip. How can you pay for that kind of craftsmanship?

I was summoned for jury duty this month. Dozens of Stafford citizens are gently asked by the sheriff and clerk of court to do their duty. We waited approximately two hours to see if the trial would occur (finally, an agreement was reached by the attorneys). During the wait, my fellow jurors and I were able to watch the First Sergeant Lindsay Truslow jury duty stand-up routine. As Lindsay explains the circuit court process, he peppers his comments with observations about human nature and jokes about lawyers. Few of us came to jury duty looking forward to the experience, and everyone left with a smile on his face.

Good customer service is simply one person through actions and words telling his fellow human being "I value you and I will do what I can to help you." The Lindsay Truslow stand-up show is one of many countless examples where county staff enrich the lives of our residents just by being yourselves. Fast and cheap is nice. But the old cliché still rings true—it's the thought that counts.

And yes, I know carrot cake is not a healthy snack.

Thanks for all you do.

NOVEMBER 2010

COLD ham on buttered bread.

That's one of my most powerful Thanksgiving memories.

When I lived in Southern California as a child, my family headed to my uncle's Newport Beach house for Thanksgiving. My aunt prepared a traditional meal of turkey, ham, and all the trimmings. After we had stuffed ourselves until our pants could hold no more, we would leave the table and head to the family room where my college-age cousins would sing Beach Boy tunes. Marty would play the guitar while Eric and Jan kept the harmony. Eric was a trained operatic tenor, so his renditions of Beach Boy hits were especially interesting to hear. They would start with "Help Me Rhonda," then go to "Barbara Anne" (enhanced by Marty's falsetto) and then sing "Fun, Fun, Fun." Eric and Marty would finish with their all-male duo of "In My Room."

Then it was time for a Thanksgiving tradition—the annual channel 5 Thanksgiving *Twilight Zone* marathon. (In the early 1980s, Los Angeles had an amazing five TV channels!) With bulging bellies, we would sit nearly comatose watching the giant woman bat away the tiny spaceman and the gremlin on the plane's wing that only William Shatner sees.

By then, it was dusk and time for the second course. My aunt would take white bread, slather it with real butter, and add ham slices. Even though we were still full from lunch, those sandwiches were some of the best-tasting food I would ever eat.

When it was time to go, we hated to leave and couldn't wait until next year. We left with a full stomach, humming "In My Room."

As a child, I never thought much of what it took for my aunt to prepare two huge meals for fifteen people. I didn't know what effort it took to set the table, prepare the bird and all the side dishes, wash all the china by hand, and return it to the china cabinet for its next long-awaited use. She always smiled, never complained, and seemed to take great pleasure in stuffing each of us to the brink.

A fellow county employee recently observed that in surviving this recession, the extra hours and effort that used to be *appreciated* are now simply *expected*. Perhaps we need to take a step back and reinforce our efforts toward gratitude. While I hardly take note of a "thank you" from a friend or colleague, I almost always remember the absence of one. Gratitude and appreciation are part of the glue that holds together an organization or a family. Genuine gratitude is both free and priceless.

To this day, I wonder if I had been more appreciative if my aunt would have let me stay over for breakfast.

For the daily miracles you do for the people of Stafford and your fellow employees, I say this:

Thanks for all you do.

DECEMBER 2010

CHRISTMAS is almost here, and I have nothing to put together.

For those first few Christmases since the kids were born, I assembled Santa's toys on Christmas Eve. Late on December 24, I would cut into the boxes and put together the motorcycle, the wagon, or the dollhouse. The assembly would go well into Christmas morning. The assembly instructions were always in pictures or German and never consisted of less than thirty-seven steps to the finish. If the final product looked similar to its photo on the box and there were less than five pieces unused in assembly, I declared victory and placed the toy by the tree. I used eggnog and choice words (not appropriate for Yuletide cheer) to get the job done. As the kids grew older, I got smarter and started assembly a couple of nights before Christmas Eve.

This year, our youngest is seven years old, and the kids' Christmas lists include tiny electronic devices, books, Pillow Pets, and gift cards to Aeropostale, Hollister, and Target. We have no ride-on trains. No Fisher-Price Harley-Davidson. No Thomas trains. No fake bugs or reptiles. When they open the iPod on Christmas morning, they don't need Dad's help. And there's just no help I can offer at Aeropostale. Why does everything have to be so tight?

I am a Christmas relic. My once essential "Dad Assembly" role relegated to only "January Bill Payer." The expert organizational development consultant would demand that I rethink my role in our family organization. Perhaps through adaptive theory application, I may continue to fulfill a value-added role in the evolving Romanello Christmas household. Maybe I can cook Christmas breakfast?

Like those marathon Christmas Eve assembly sessions, many of you are toiling countless hours to meet the needs of our great community. I hope that you are able to take a moment and reflect on the gifts you give our community through your work.

I will likely be asleep at 1:00 a.m. this Christmas Eve. What I would give to be knee-deep in Styrofoam and picture book instructions! If you have little children in need of Santa's assembly services, I am available. My wrench is warmed up. My screwdriver is ready to turn. I promise to use as many of the pieces as I can.

Thanks for all you do. And may God bless us, every one.

JANUARY 2011

MARY'S friend had her birthday party at the Cavalier roller skating rink. I was a little early to pick up Mary, so I had the chance to watch the place. Soon, I was taken back to my middle school years.

I could never roller skate, but I wouldn't miss a skate night because everybody went. One birthday, my aunt bought me a pair of brown suede roller skates. While my feet looked snazzy, I still hugged the wall so as not to injure myself or others.

Once the disco ball was lit, the rink was filled with middle schoolers rolling around at high speeds to "Thriller," "Jump," or "She Blinded Me with Science." Girls traveled in packs giggling and pretending to ignore the boys. Boys traveled singularly, each trying to impress the girls with his roller skating tricks. Most of my talented friends missed the opportunity of sympathy. Like an injured puppy, my pathetic lack of skating talent would have girls saying, "Aw, at least he's trying." The girls barely noticed the boys doing tricks with one foot in the air.

When we took a break from skating, we drank Cokes, ate Jujyfruits, and played Pac Man and Galaga until our fingers hurt. As 9:00 p.m. approached and skate night was ending, we prayed our parents would park deep in the parking lot and let us come to them. But inevitably, my dad would park his car in the fire lane right outside the front door. Like the criminal defendant facing TV cameras, I had to slither into the car in great embarrassment.

Mary wakes me from my daydream: "Dad, I'm ready to go." I realized that I was gently shaking my hips to some indiscernibly loud tune by Ke$ha. Now awakened from my memory, I thought to myself, *My back really hurts*.

For just a few minutes, I was given the gift of a powerful and wonderful daydream. Surely in this rough and tumble world, we have enough reality to keep us busy. When an event or a song or a smell triggers a great memory, it can be a moment to savor. Kids dream all the time—we call it imagination. I wonder if we adults dream enough. Maybe instead of staff meetings, we should have "imagination meetings"?

When I finished middle school and those brown suede roller skates no longer fit, we took them to Goodwill. I hoped their new owner would take them out for a high speed skate and dance in a figure-8 around the rink.

When I pick up my kids now, I usually park inconspicuously deep in the parking lot. But sometimes, just for fun, I wait for them in the fire lane just as my dad did.

Thanks for all you do.

MARCH 2011

I never met Travis.

He died in December at the age of twenty-five. Cystic fibrosis took him.

Travis's dad and I have been friends and colleagues for over a decade. Travis's funeral was attended by several hundred people. His many college friends eulogized him. A line of young adults told stories of their friend's care and concern. They told whenever they would mention a movie or book that was of interest to them, Travis would immediately get it for them. They told of his love for the guitar, tennis, and for great movies. And, amazingly, they told how very few of his close friends knew of his disease. Travis was modest in his own suffering and anything but in his care for others.

The best story of the funeral came from a young lady who worked where Travis played tennis. They struck up a fast friendship and talked of their favorite movies. Last Valentine's Day, Travis invited her to his house. When she arrived, he gave her candy and flowers and then said, "Let's go." They drove to Richmond's Byrd Theatre, a 1920s vintage movie palace. They walked into the empty theater, and Travis told her to pick any seat. The two sat in this enormous theater for a private screening of her favorite movie. After she told this story, every woman at the funeral was weeping and every man in the church, reminded of his dating years, thought, *I wish I had thought of that!*

That was Travis, not just generous, but creatively giving to all of those around him.

I had lunch with his dad this week who told me that he and his wife had not heard most of the stories about Travis until the funeral. They have watched the DVD of the funeral several times to learn more about their wonderful son. In his short twenty-five years, Travis touched enough lives for a century of living.

We touch the lives of our children, spouses, parents, and coworkers through daily acts of dedication, service, and love. Yet when we think of them, we remember specific acts where they gave all for us, when they stood up for us even when we were wrong, or when they made us laugh uncontrollably. It takes only a moment to touch someone's life.

I never met Travis. Thanks to the lives he touched, I do know him.

Thanks for all you do.

April 2011

THIS week, I met Savannah. She wants to change the world.

Savannah is six years old.

Keenly interested in the environment, Savannah organized a Recess Club at Anne E. Moncure Elementary School to pick up trash around the school playground. Her birthday is in August, so she doesn't get to be with her classmates on her birthday. So she and her mom organized a spring party. Instead of going to Chuck E. Cheese or Fun Land, on the first day of spring, Savannah had her spring party at Aquia Landing. She and her friends patrolled the beach and filled bags with the trash that blows into the park.

The spring party would be a well-kept secret except on that same day, our own MC Moncure was at the park. Earlier this week, MC and I visited Savannah's first-grade classroom with cupcakes for her and her friends. Savannah now wears proudly a Stafford County lapel pin in recognition of her efforts.

Historians, political scientists, and anthropologists consider the question: what does it take to change the world? The answer would be simpler for them if they were to meet Savannah.

Can we change the world with an army of first-graders

picking up trash? Savannah thinks so. And after sharing a cupcake with this beautiful little girl, I agree.

Amazing how a child can impact the world.

Thanks for all you do.

MAY 2011

MARY'S fifth-grade skate night ended early when a couple of aggressive boys dominoed her to the hard floor. She fractured her wrist on the way down. She cried with pain until the good folks at Stafford Hospital gave her a splint and some codeine. A couple of days later, the orthopedist determined surgery was necessary to reset the bones to heal permanently.

The surgery requires a general anesthesia; moving bones back into place will cause great pain in even the most courageous of patients. As many times as I have gone under, the thought of my daughter going under was really scary. With four kids, we've had our share of ER trips, but nobody had gone under yet.

The surgery day came, and Mary lay in the hospital bed. She was wired to the heart monitor, with the pulse oxygen indicator on her finger and IV line stuck in her arm. The nurse assured me they do thirty of these every day, but I didn't care about the other twenty-nine! In that hospital bed, Mary wasn't my eleven-year-old fifth grader. She was that little two-year-old girl with ringlets. With the "happy juice" administered, Mary faded and was sent to surgery.

Less than thirty minutes later, the doctor came out to tell us the surgery was successfully completed. I was relieved and felt silly for being so anxious. Mary's modest surgery experience made me appreciate more the experiences of parents whose children are gravely ill. Given the opportunity, who among us wouldn't trade places with our sick or hurt child?

In public service, we sometimes find ourselves helping people when they are most vulnerable. The compassion and competence we show is a form of human anesthesia to help them through their situation. These are the daily miracles that call us to public service.

There is more good news from Mary's experience. Since she was born, I have told her to stay away from boys. With roller-skating boys breaking her wrist, she has real life evidence that her dad is right.

Thanks for all you do.

JUNE 2011

DON'T let my kids read this.

Sometimes it's hard to communicate with teenagers. When I ask my sons about their day or the latest happenings at school, I receive one-word answers: "okay," "fine," or "lame." It's as if they have been advised by their defense attorney to keep their answers brief for fear of future reprisal.

But then there's texting . . .

We decided to wait until ninth grade to provide our kids with cell phones. They remind us frequently that *all* their friends received cell phones as soon as they were potty trained. The kids argue that texting is not just a communication enhancement, but a First Amendment right. When the first phone was purchased, I protested "unlimited" texting asking, "How much do you really use that stuff?" They laughed out loud at me.

But, you see, here's the thing. Where there are one-word verbal answers, I receive a rich commentary through texting. It's short, curiously abbreviated, and full of code words. But my kids are telling me their story in their own way. Sentences become acronyms. Words become single letters. What texting lacks in grammar and spelling, it gains in heart and honesty. In a sense, my move to their way of communicating is no different from when they were little and I would get on my knees to talk eye to eye with them.

I still argue that face-to-face is the ideal form of communication, and there are those rare moments certainly when the kids will sit and talk (cell phone vibrating throughout the conversation). But in between those rare gifts, texting helps us communicate "eye to eye." The important thing is that we are communicating and sharing our lives.

As we serve the public, we are challenged daily to enhance our communications. Often, communication is more than the written or spoken word: it can be through body language or a simple smile. To secularize the great philosopher priest Francis of Assisi, "Communicate often and use words when necessary."

Please don't tell my kids they are communicating with their dad.

Tx4aludo.

August 2011

MY favorite birthday gift this year was a recipe book. My sister compiled our mother's favorite recipes: manicotti, ravioli, crumb coffee cake, biscotti, gingerbread, and numerous others. The book includes vintage 1960s newspaper recipes, dog-eared pages from the Betty Crocker cookbook, and recipes written in my mother's own hand. Her handwriting flows elegantly across the page and reflects the careful effort required by the nuns who taught her how to write in the late 1930s.

When I first saw the pages written in my mother's hand, I was overcome with emotion. *I realized this was the first time I had seen my mother's handwriting.* I lost my mom when I was two years old.

It seemed silly to be so affected by a cookbook.

About a month later, I attended a class where the lecturer was talking on the subject of connection among people. He spoke, in particular, about visceral, instinctive memories. He noted our most vivid memories are not cognitive—they are physical. This certainly made sense to me. Sometimes, a scent or a texture brings back an old memory.

At the end of the lecture, I asked the professor why I was so overcome with emotion by the cookbook. He explained that while my mom died when I was two and I have no cognitive memories of her, I have two years of powerful, visceral memories of my mother. Even though I didn't "know" it, I remember my mother. Her handwriting stirred those visceral memories in me.

My life changed when he said to me, "Anthony, every cell of your body has the physical imprint of the memory of your mother."

I had been searching for a memory of my mother for thirty-nine years. She was with me all the time.

Her manicotti will be more delicious than ever.

Thanks for all you do.

SEPTEMBER 2011

I go to see my favorite tree a few times a year.

The tree sits in front of our former home on Fitzhugh Avenue in West Richmond. The City of Richmond had an Adopt-a-Tree program where residents could pay for street trees, and the city would plant a tree in front of your home.

Richmond's streets are lined with huge trees, many planted decades ago. Walnuts, pecans, oaks, and cherries shade the sidewalks and the travel lanes. Their massive roots lift up the asphalt in the street and the concrete in the sidewalk. Some of the more notable trees have been preserved by routing the sidewalk in a semicircular fashion around their roots. We were advised by the city arborist that a Japanese zelkova was a perfect street tree—fast growing with a good shade canopy and roots that tended to grow down instead of out so they won't rip up the sidewalk. Our zelkova was green in the spring and summer and turned to brilliant fall hues in the autumn.

The tree was planted in the first week of October, just a few days after John, our oldest, was born. It has always been John's tree. At first, the two looked somewhat alike. The zelkova was a scrawny sapling held vertical by a wooden stake. Born weighing over eight pounds, John had trouble feeding in his first month; and by Halloween, he was scrawny too. (He will be sixteen next week, and his six daily meals today make up for his early feeding problems).

We moved when the tree was only five years old, so most of the tree's beautiful years have been enjoyed by the people who lived in the house after us. So it is true with many trees. Countless times, I have driven down Grove Avenue in West Richmond to enjoy the early fall show of spectacular yellows, oranges, and reds. Most of those trees were planted before World War II. Their planters have long since moved away, yet we all are able to enjoy them.

A Chinese proverb says that the best time to plant a tree was twenty years ago and the next best time is now. What saplings can we plant in our daily lives that will give beauty and hope to those who come after us? We plant the seeds of goodwill every day and cultivate them with our commitment to public service.

Fall is here. The leaves on John's tree are about to turn. I can't wait to see it again.

Thanks for all you do.

OCTOBER 2011

MY favorite Halloween costume was a superhero with no comic book or TV show to call his own.

In my childhood mind, no one superhero was sufficient, so I created my own. He was called Super A and could fly like Superman, swim like Aquaman, and solve thorny dilemmas with a wit as keen as Batman's. Super A had two simple purposes in life. The first, of course, was to save the world. The second purpose was to win Wonder Woman's heart.

To become Super A, I donned a red sweater with a yellow felt *A* clipped to my chest. A wool blanket was my cape. A black Lone Ranger mask covered my face, and I wore tight sweatpants over my legs (my apologies for the image you now have in your mind). While Super A saved the world from the brink of total annihilation numerous times, he had no such luck with Wonder Woman (perhaps it was the outfit?).

What child, adolescent, and young adult doesn't see himself saving the world? But as we mature, our aspirations temper, and we grow to understand that while we may not save the world by doing purposeful work, we make the world a better place.

The 2008 Stafford tornado that affected nearly 150 families occurred a few days before Mother's Day. While

I am exceedingly proud of our efforts at response and recovery in the England Run North neighborhood, one of my fondest memories is Mother's Day morning. County staff provided flowers, cards, and donated gift cards to the kids whose homes were damaged. While their lives were turned upside down, all these moms were able to celebrate Mother's Day.

Whether it's a simple flower, a critical report, or a life-saving rescue, all aspects of our work have purpose. Every encounter is an opportunity to serve. While the larger purpose of our work may not be self-evident in the moment, over time, these daily miracles of service to our customers and to each other cultivate the seeds that grow a great community. Only a few in human history are called to save the world, but all of us are called to build a great community.

I love the story of the man on a walk who comes across a sparrow lying in the middle of the road. The bird is on his back with his legs straight in the air. The man asks the bird what he is doing. The bird says, "The sky is falling." The man replies, "You crazy bird! The sky is falling, and you think those little legs will hold it up?" The bird says, "You are right. I can't do it alone, but I can do my part."

I like to think of our Stafford County team as sparrows performing daily miracles to build a great community. No superheroes needed.

Thanks for all you do.

DECEMBER 2011

M Y backyard has the best Christmas tree in the world.

It's taller than the national tree at the White House and more festive than Rockefeller Center's. Its colored lights make a kaleidoscope beacon throughout South Stafford. People come from miles just to see it.

Well, not really.

Our yard Christmas tree is about three feet tall. While Stafford's acidic soil scares away blades of grass in my backyard, this little tree dares to grow on the steep slope. Last summer as a scrub pine, it barely missed the teeth of the lawnmower. I protected the sapling with bricks at its base and promised to decorate it when it grew to a proper size. But I couldn't wait.

Last weekend, my girls and I adorned it with pink, green, orange, and blue lights that make its wispy branches sag from the weight, like a little boy dressed in his dad's overcoat.

I can't stop looking at it. I can't wait for dark so we can see its lights again. What wonderful daydreams that little tree brings.

I am reminded of childhood Christmases when our family tree towered over me and the angel on top seemed to be miles away. I think about that Christmas when I received my first Victorinox Swiss Army knife with its corkscrew, toothpick, and two knife blades that I was sure would help me take on the world. I remember the devastation of the most dreaded Christmas gift of every boy—sweaters! I think back to Intellivision baseball and Lock-n-Chase video games. My first Sears Craftsman screwdriver set with its many Phillips head and slotted options enabled my adolescent friends and me to open a bike repair business.

Now in my middle years, I marvel at how this little sapling has the audacity to grow in the grass-less soil among the backdrop of sixty-foot tall hardwoods. Surely, I can imagine its future as a towering evergreen with long thick branches. And while its future height and beauty are exciting to consider, I am most impressed by the character and aspirations it has today.

Last summer's weed is now the world's best Christmas tree. Its glow reminds me that the most cherished things in life aren't things.

Thanks for all you do. And may God bless us, every one.

JANUARY 2012

JOHN, our oldest, has his driver's license.

He drove our other car behind me recently. As I looked at him in the rearview mirror, I couldn't help thinking of that little boy wearing a Mickey Mouse sweater on his first birthday. Didn't we just bring him home from the hospital? And I know he's made me watch *Winnie the Pooh* three times this week.

Blink once and he will have graduated college. Blink again, and he will have a wife and his own son.

Both Stafford High School and the Commonwealth of Virginia tell me he's qualified to drive. Yet when I hand him the car keys, I don't see a sixteen-year-old young man. I see a little boy with a fat orange whiffle ball bat begging "Just one more pitch, Dad, please."

We kept his fingers out of light sockets and strapped him into his car seat like an astronaut. We celebrated the last bottle of formula and cheered the final diaper. How I wish I could trade those car keys for a bottle of Enfamil!

Letting go is hard. But one has to release, or at least loosen, the ties that bind. No tulip bulb brightens our day until it punches through the earth to weather the early spring storms. No bird soars inside his nest. No child grows unless we let him.

After multiple duct tape repairs, I had to throw away the orange whiffle ball bat. Letting go is hard.

Thanks for all you do.

MARCH 2012

THIS is Stafford's Baby Boom.

I can't remember a time when more of our team members were pregnant. Over the next several months, the *Watercooler* will be filled with pictures of new lives among us.

As I've talked to the moms, a few want to be surprised by the gender, but everyone wants to know the *quantity* of babies she is having.

I admire those I know whose children are grown and living good lives as adults. They are the gurus of parenting. I am a "rookie" parent with only sixteen years' experience, so I offer my observations from the first few seasons on the parenting field of play:

- Never throw away an old towel. You will be cleaning up lots of . . . stuff.
- You think you'll save money when you stop buying formula and diapers. You won't. Something more costly will come along.
- Whether they're listening or not, kids hear everything we say and forget little. (Significant exceptions: Take out the trash. Clean your room. Leave your muddy shoes in the garage).
- With one or two children, the man-to-man

defense works well. With three or more, try the zone defense. When the zone defense doesn't work, bring in grandparents or neighbors. For extreme situations, call Ben & Jerry.

- If you chill Yoo Hoo, Hawaiian Punch, or blue Mountain Dew in your garage refrigerator, the kids will come—lots of them.

- While the teenage years are hard for parents, they're even harder on the teenager.

- When they're too old to hold your hand, remember they need to hold on to you, in their own way, even harder.

- Grades, merit badges, talent shows, base hits, and piano recitals make you proud, but what really gives you that lump in your throat is when your child lifts up another through exercising his/her character.

The members of our Stafford family coming this year will never see an incandescent light bulb. Hard copies of *Encyclopaedia Britannica* will be found only in museums. iPads will be to them what eight-track cassettes are to us. They will graduate high school in 2030. I know these new little souls will make the world a better place because their moms are doing so today.

New moms and dads: save all your old towels. The rest—somehow, some way—just works out.

Thanks for all you do.

APRIL 2012

I have a new place in our county add to my list of favorites—Abel Lake Reservoir.

Last week, I walked the dam at the Abel Lake Water Reservoir. Built in 1970, Abel Lake is one year younger than its brother reservoir at Smith Lake. Abel is the water source for most of South Stafford and is fed by Potomac Creek and all the streams, ditches, and roof gutters that drain to the creek. Abel holds 1.3 billion gallons of water compared to Smith's 2.1 billion. Plant manager Matt Sauter and his able team provide forty-thousand people safe, clean, and great-tasting water, every day of the year. Abel Lake and Smith's younger brother, Rocky Pen Run Reservoir, will be the family overachiever when it is born in 2014, weighing in at 5.4 billion gallons.

Covered with lush green grass, the Abel dam is an earthen structure. Through the bottom of the dam snakes a concrete pipe to control the flow of water. The top of the dam is probably about fifty feet wide (upstream to downstream). Straddling the dam are steep grassy slopes known as emergency spillways. These allow water to flow around the dam in major storm and hurricane events. Both spillways protected the dam in the torrents of Hurricane Agnes in 1972.

When we toured the dam, it was a perfect spring

day—warm and sunny with a breeze. We climbed the tall grass of the dam, and when we reached the top, I was out of breath from the natural "stair climber." Standing at the top, panting for air, I was able to peer out at both the lake and the downstream "stilling pond." I learned a stilling pond is a rip rap (large stone) filled-area that is used to slow down fast-moving water before it returns to the natural creek.

The view is spectacular. While the top of the dam is only twenty-seven-feet vertically from the pool of water, I felt I was standing on a mountain.

I tried to soak in the view as best I could. I thought about taking a picture with my phone, but didn't. It was one of those moments best remembered by my senses. No medium could capture the coarse grass against my legs, the blowing breeze, the 360-degree horizon of trees, and the dribbling water from the under-dam channel to the stilling pool.

I didn't want to leave. For a few minutes in the middle of a busy day, it was utter peace.

Wouldn't it be something if all our life's floods could be contained with emergency spillways? Or when man-made storms bring frustration and anger, what if we were able to enter a stilling pool until we collect ourselves to rejoin family or colleagues to give them our best? Imagine, if just once in a while, we could stand at a great height and view our world from all sides. Dam, that would be cool.

Thanks for all you do.

MAY 2012

GRACE is the ubiquitous image seen in restaurants, hotels, and dining rooms all over America. Minnesota photographer Eric Enstrom took *Grace* in black and white in 1918 when an itinerant peddler visited his studio.

Later, the image was refashioned into the the sepia-toned picture common today. Even if you don't know the name of the photograph, it seems obvious the old man is praying before his meal.

Or is he?

I love to pull this picture off the wall and ask people, "What's he thinking?" Here's some options that come to mind:

- Soup and bread again!
- The life of an itinerant peddler is tough; I don't how I will make ends meet. My worries have my mind so upside down. I put the bread on the table with no plate!
- Do I really need a knife that large to cut a loaf of bread? Why did I place the knife on the table with the sharp edge pointed to myself? And my elbows barely touch the table. Why am I so apprehensive?

- I'm hot. Look at that summer sun shining in through the window. Why did I wear a flannel shirt on a summer day?
- I am so bored. Albert, sitting at the other end of this table, is so long-winded. The longer I pray, the longer I can postpone his tiresome chatter.
- This great beard surely will fill with soup remnants. I wish I had a napkin.
- What's in that book will answer my concerns. If I point the lens of my glasses into its contents, will my eyes absorb its wisdom?
- I wish this guy would hurry and take the picture. I am really hungry.

When asked, with time for reflection, "What's he thinking?" rich responses can come. Kids are especially fun with this exercise.

With a passing glance, we see a man praying before his meal. When asked to concentrate on the photograph, we realize there could be much more to this scene. And when we come back to it after reflection, we discover new possibilities.

How often do we give only passing glances to those we see daily? If we gave those around us the gift of careful reflection, what possibilities would we see in them?

Thanks for all you do.

June 2012

S HINING eyes.
I love to see shining eyes. Benjamin Zander, conductor of the Boston Philharmonic, coined the term *shining eyes* as the moment when possibility is awakened in us. When possibility is awakened, the face lights up and the eyes shine.

Like *Alice in Wonderland*'s White Queen who "dreams of six impossible things before breakfast," possibility is second nature for children. Kids' eyes shine when given a fresh coloring book and a box of Crayolas, when they spot a gigantic Moon Bounce, or when that favorite song comes on the radio for the ninety-seventh time.

For us adults, shining eyes are rare. The vagaries of everyday life allow reality to limit possibility. In our quest to focus on the tasks at hand, we may even discipline ourselves for daydreaming. But every once in a while, possibility escapes its workaday trap, and our eyes shine. And it's a great moment to watch.

Sometimes, it's obvious. A colleague will say, "I have an idea," and her lit eyes clue into the possibilities about to come. More often, however, it's more subtle as the person I'm listening to doesn't even realize his words move from the reality realm to the possibility realm. His face fills with light and excitement, and the pace of his talking quickens. First person language goes away as he talks of great things *we* can accomplish and how to move *the county* to the next level. He can't conceal the smile on his face as the fire hose of optimism sprays possibilities into the conversation.

As the shining eyes talk, I find myself focusing more on the exuberance and less on the words. And I can't help smiling and be infected by the optimism of possibility.

Imagine the possibilities if we think only *one* impossible thing each day. Please pass the Crayolas.

Thanks for all you do.

JULY 2012

DO you know what your first word was?
Most of us begin to speak before we are one-year old, and as we do, we learn intent with our language. As our communication shifts from crying and gesturing, we begin to use words with intent to get what we want or need.

Some children with disabilities can say words but cannot communicate with the words. For example, they may see a ball and say "ball" but cannot say "ball" to communicate "I want the ball" or "Look at the ball."

My wife, Diane, teaches such young children. She worked recently with a two-and-a-half-year-old boy. To teach him word *intent*, she uses a word he can already say—*ball*—and holds the ball for him to see. He cannot have the ball until he says the word. She models the game with the mother showing the child what is expected, encourages him to imitate the word, and rewards his language attempts with the ball. In between Diane's home visits, the child's parents repeat the lesson. This activity is frustrating for the child and difficult for the family. With a teenage athlete who wants to sleep instead of getting up for 5:00 a.m. winter workouts, you can motivate with the old "No Pain No Gain" cliché. With a two-and-a-half-year-old child, there is no such consolation for his frustration of a toy denied. It's hard work.

After much practice, the lessons paid off. At one recent visit, the little boy ran to his mother, gave her a wonderful hug, and said, "Momma." It was the first time in his two and a half years of life that he said "momma." The bear hug made his intent unmistakable.

Until Diane told me this story, it never occurred to me that a disability may cause us to not connect words with intent. Speaking with intent is like breathing for most of us, something you have to do but give very little thought to doing.

What a gift it is to be able to communicate to those around us in a way that clearly reflects our care, intent, and concern for them. A simple phrase can inspire or despair. A word can lift up or put down. I will use this old but newly discovered gift as wisely as I can.

A little boy goes through exhaustive lessons and finds his "momma." What a gift.

Thanks for all you do.

September 2012

Does the flap of butterfly's wing in Brazil change the weather in Texas?

S O asked Edward Lorenz in his 1963 study on the analysis of the "sensitive dependence on initial conditions." Tiny variations amplified over time, like a butterfly's wing flapping, can be a cause for a great wind far away. He called it the Butterfly Effect. This is why today's weather forecasts are in percentages of likelihood (i.e., 50 percent chance of rain) as the slightest condition in the air can change the course of weather.

Such a great wind blew through Stafford recently when citizen Buddy Secor addressed the Board of Supervisors.

Buddy was cutting his grass and suffered a heart attack. He credits his life to the excellent and collaborative work of the paramedics, sheriff's deputies, 911 telecommunicators, and medical staff at Stafford Hospital. He thanked the Board of Supervisors for their commitment to good service and ended his presentation with the ultimate in gratitude saying simply, "Thank you for my life."

If you ever wondered if the work we do is important, Buddy Secor answers a resounding "yes."

When did our help to Buddy Secor start? It began

well before his wife dialed 911. Did it start the day that
HR helped Sheriff and Fire and Rescue select quality
employees to start their academies? Did it start the day
that Finance helped purchase the ambulance or when
IT kept our aging technology functioning to ensure
communications? Did it start the day our first responders
answered the call to public service? Maybe it began with
teaching by a great teacher in the classroom or by a great
parent in the family room? You might say the butterfly's
wings were flapping for years before Buddy's fateful day.

We build a great community through our collective
efforts to create the climate for excellence and service.
Excellent service is the manifestation of thousands of
hours of training, planning, conversation, and commitment that lead to a single act. Most overnight successes
are years in the making.

When touring a NASA facility in the 1960s, President
Lyndon Johnson came across a custodian. He asked the
man what his role was at NASA. The custodian said, "Mr.
President, my job is to put a man on the moon."

Like the gentle flutter of a butterfly's wing can build
to a great wind over time, there are no small acts in public
service.

Thanks for all you do.

OCTOBER 2012

I am colorblind.

I can see colors but have trouble differentiating and identifying them. I can see all the hues of fall in the leaves. Just don't ask me to identify their colors. I learn to get by through association. The American flag is red, white, and blue. Coke cans are red. Traffic lights are red on top and green on the bottom. Cities with horizontal traffic signals can make driving interesting!

I discovered I was colorblind in elementary school when I failed a test. We were asked to fill in certain colors, and some of the old Crayolas had lost their label indicating color. So I guessed—wrongly. Soon after, my dreams were dashed as colorblind folks cannot become astronauts or fighter pilots. I chose the only slightly less glamorous profession of public administration.

Charts and graphs are the worst. The noncolorblind majority prides themselves on their multislice pie charts adorned with twelve shades of red. As they point out the difference between periwinkle, crimson, scarlet, magenta, and raspberry, we color-challenged folks find ourselves hearing not their presentation but the unintelligible "wonk, wonk, wonk, wonk, wonk" like the voice of adults in the old Charlie Brown TV specials.

Clothes can be tough also, so the white shirt is my

best friend. I thought one of my favorite pair of shorts was orange, until after three years, I was told they were hot pink. (They went to Goodwill).

When I brown sausage to add to my marinara sauce, I have to have one of my kids tell me that all the pink is gone. (Warning: eating food prepared by us colorblind folks may be risky).

Certainly colorblindness is really only a pesky inconvenience, and I am grateful for it. People who are not colorblind find our malady so peculiar. As I explain to them what it's like to be colorblind, I am reminded that we all see the world in different ways. Our world is definitely not black and white, and what some may see as crimson red, others see as hunter green.

Those autumn leaves sure are beautiful—whatever color they may be.

Thanks for all you do.

NOVEMBER 2012

I T was bedtime the day after Thanksgiving when Anna came to me crying.

I looked for signs of blood or injury, but there was none. I asked, "What's wrong?"

She said, "I don't know. I'm just sad."

My thoughts raced in panic. *Diane and the rest of the family aren't home. Injuries, I can handle. I can get to the ER in record time! But nine-year-old-girl's sadness, there's no guidebook on how to handle this. Do the guys at 1-800-DADHELP work on the holiday weekend? Perhaps Google has the answer? You can handle this, Anthony.*

I held her for a while and then sent her off to get dressed for bed. I thought the distraction of a book would help, so I suggested she read. In an hour, she seemed herself again. I tucked her in, and she went right to sleep.

The next morning I asked her if she was feeling better. Anna said, "Yes, I don't know why I was sad. I just needed to cry."

When someone is crying, we are conditioned to think "I wonder what's wrong." Crying is one of our body's release valves. Anxiety, tension, and hurt feelings are dampened through our eye's salty leakage. For some, this release is as frequent as the April rain and easily summoned by a sentimental song or story. For others, it may rain in the desert more than tears hit our face. Regardless of our personal climate, Anna Romanello's prescription for what ails us is a good cry.

Anna didn't need the well-worn "life's not fair" Dad-speech. No Band-Aid was required either. She just needed to cry.

Thanks for all you do.

DECEMBER 2012

TWENTY-SEVEN angels are calling.

After an unimaginable morning in Newton, Connecticut, these angels summon us.

Many of us will ask *how* or *why* or *who's responsible for this atrocity? Certainly this could have been prevented*, we may say. We will suggest *it is a failure of security or mental health systems*. Laying blame is a temporary elixir to reduce the pain of the grief we all share. But as the tempering effect of laying blame wears off, we are left with questions unanswered and holes in our hearts.

So while we may never have the consolation of answers to *who's responsible, why*, and *how*, we can answer one question—*what can I do next?* In light of this horrifying darkness, what can I do next to lift up another soul? In the wake of this evil of evils, what I can do next to serve my fellow man?

Is there a greater tribute to these twenty-seven souls than to ask ourselves *what can I do next* and to act on that answer?

We say public service is a calling. Twenty-seven voices beckon.

Thanks for all you do. And may God bless us, everyone.

February 2013

ONE hit a week.

That's what it takes to improve from a .250 to a .300 hitter according to *Bull Durham*'s Crash Davis. A good major league player will have a .250 batting average (twenty-five hits in every one hundred at bats). A player who hits .300 over his career will, most likely, earn a spot in the hall of fame.

When I first heard Crash's advice, I didn't believe it. Could it be that only one more hit per week takes you from average to hall of fame? I did my own Excel spreadsheet—and sure enough, Crash is correct.

The world of retail self-improvement presents before and after pictures of people completely transformed. They lose fifty pounds in a month, learn a foreign language in days, or earn millions in weeks. Perhaps a few of these transformations do happen, but most of us give up soon after trying because the grand transformation seems unreachable.

Quick change rarely endures. Lasting change comes in the fullness of time. After all, a rock is shined at the bottom of a stream not by the quick rushing flood but by the gentle polishing-years of slow-moving water. Its transformation is so gradual that we assume it's always been that beautiful.

That one extra hit a week doesn't need to be pretty. A nubber over the shortstop's head into shallow left field counts the same as a three-run blast to center—a hit is a hit.

Philosopher William James must have been playing with Crash when he wrote,

> I am done with great things and big plans, great institutions and big successes. I am for those tiny, invisible loving human forces that work from individual to individual, creeping through the crannies of the world like so many rootlets, or like the capillary oozing of water, yet which, if given time, will rend the hardest monuments of human pride.

Keep swinging.
Thanks for all you do.

MARCH 2013

I T was well after midnight, and I couldn't sleep.
In the adjoining room of the hotel where I was staying,
a baby's cry pierced through the wafer-thin walls. As a
veteran parent, I knew the fast and desperate cry was a
hungry cry, different from the unmistakable scream of a
finger caught in the door or the agitated pleading caused
by a damp diaper.

I had an early start that next morning, so I was mad.
Who travels with a baby? How could they let that baby
cry so? I'm sure they're negotiating whose turn it is to
wake up. And those penny-pinching corporate executives,
couldn't they put soundproofing in the walls? After 2:00
a.m., a quiet stillness came. My anger gave way to exhaustion, and I slept.

Just before 6:00 a.m., the crying resumed. It was fast,
desperate, and hungry, but in my sleep-deprived stupor,
the cries seemed to be not from an annoying baby in the
next hotel room, but the cry of one of my own children. I
lay in bed with the crying reminding me how much I miss
the zombie-walk to the kitchen to get a bottle ready. What
I would give for a tired little person to rub his eyes with
tiny fingers or lay her head on my shoulder. And there's
no better sleep than that with a swaddled child at peace,
curled up on my chest, and a tilted bottle dripping formula

on the chair. Sure, those sleepless weeks with a newborn seem interminable. And I never appreciated fully a good night's rest until we had children. It's been over nine years since my last middle of the night feeding, and today, I wish I could put a bottle in their mouths rather than car keys in their hands.

The people next door were more efficient in the early morning hours than at night. My little next-door neighbor's cries ended soon after they started. *Too bad,* I thought, *I could have listened to that baby for hours.*

How did a midnight irritation become a wonderful gift at 6:00 a.m.? Did the tired frustration of the dark night give way to the joyful anticipation of the new day? Or was my four hours' rest between my neighbor's feedings a reminder that lost sleep—whether giving a bottle to a baby or watching bad TV until the teenager gets home late at night—is job one for every parent?

The things in life we dislike may become, in hindsight, among our favorite memories.

The next time I check in to a hotel, I may just ask for a room adjoining a baby's.

Thanks for all you do.

MAY 2013

IT was storming early one morning in Nashville. There for my nephew's graduation, I was headed out for the day's events when I met Gail. In her midfifties, Gail had a backpack on her shoulder, a nylon bag in one hand, and a plastic bag in the other, all stuffed so tight an index card couldn't be added. She needed a ride to the Belmont area of Nashville which, she explained, was only fifteen minutes away. I had forty-five minutes to make it to my nephew's graduation.

As I considered helping her, the devil on my left shoulder was fighting with the angel on my right: *Drive a complete stranger across town? Well, it is pouring down rain, and I do have the time. Are you crazy, Anthony, what if she pulls a gun on you? It's the nice thing to do. You drove all this way to Nashville, and you're going to be late to graduation?* I stifled my head voices and said to Gail, "Okay, let's go."

She lifted her three bags into the back seat and sat in the front seat. As we drove, she told me her life story pausing only to give directions and offer to cut the ride short. She could see my eyes drifting to the clock on the dashboard.

Gail is homeless and was heading to Belmont to a Methodist church that would help her with a job. She is estranged from her kids and has no family near Nashville.

As we passed the massive homes lining Belmont's streets, her story became more incredulous with details of ornate furniture stored in Canada and family members moving to Europe. Gail could sense my unease about being late, and her voice quickened with it. Like the voices in my head arguing over whether to give her a ride, Gail's story was both forlorn and hopeful.

After twenty minutes, we made it to the Methodist Church, and the rain had slowed to a drizzle. She gathered her three bags, thanked me twice, and walked to the church. She asked me for nothing.

I drove to the graduation, arriving early.

I want to feel good about driving Gail, but I don't. I wish I had pulled over the car, shut off the engine, and looked her in the eyes to listen to her story. Was her story incredulous because of its absurdity, or was it so because I was listening with one eye on the road and one eye on the clock? She asked for a taxi driver—what she really needed was a friend.

A good friend once told me every encounter is an opportunity to serve. That stormy Saturday, I was a taxi driver and an on-time uncle. I wish I had been a friend to Gail.

Thanks for all you do.

JULY 2013

I was given a great gift.
A colleague disagreed with me. I was expressing my satisfaction on a piece of work that I consider a signature accomplishment. She reflected on the same but characterized it as a lost opportunity. I thanked her for the conversation, in particular, for caring enough about what I had to say to share her viewpoint.

Disagreeing with someone is a gift. Diversity of perspective is the hallmark of a strong organization. It is harder to stir up concerned dissent than to maintain apathetic silence, so I am grateful when people take them time to offer an alternative perspective. No strong organization is fed by a daily diet of compliance and quiet assent. Curious, respectful dissent drives creativity and opens minds to new possibilities.

As we argue about *how* to get somewhere we may lose sight that, in many cases, we are headed to the same place. I am reminded of this when I Google directions. Often Google provides three different routes to the destination and even more if you are driving, walking or taking public transportation—many choices that all end up at the same place. Spirited debate doesn't mean we don't share common principles. After all, the clocks of the world's major cities may show different hours, but they all are on the same minute.

I can think of times working with a group of people where we seemed to have reached consensus, and one brave soul speaks out to challenge the group think. The false consensus is revealed, and in time, the epiphany of the lone dissenter will enlighten the room.

Concerned dissent is not anarchy. We can rock the boat without sinking the ship. It's important that our public voice be one. Our collective aim to build a great community reminds us that dissent is often a conversation about means, not ends. Concerned disagreement is a rare gift.

Imagine how strong our discourse would be if we began conversations with: *You and I are headed to the same place. Now let's talk about how we get there.*

Thanks for all you do.

AUGUST 2013

THE signs were so tempting we had to stop.

On our way to Tallahassee, my son Domenic, my daughter Anna, and I were rolling along Florida's Interstate 10. The road is flat, straight, and unremarkable except for the large Florida Citrus Center signs every few miles. The billboards show gigantic oranges extolling free samples of delicious Florida fruit and a "thirteen-foot gator." Ahead of schedule in our trip, I asked the kids if they wanted to stop to see the gator. As we closed in on the center, we began to imagine what we'd see: *Where do they keep a thirteen-foot gator? Can we fill up on fruit samples so we won't need to buy lunch?* Finally, we arrived.

The Florida Citrus Center is about the size of a 7-11 with a building and a parking lot demonstrating the owner's aim for quaint vs. modern. A man outside the store, cutting watermelon and oranges, greeted us. In front of him were small Tupperware bowls containing wafer-thin orange slices and bullion-sized watermelon cubes. A sign read "one sample per customer." We savored our little treats and went in search for the gator.

Inside was a sea of key chains, postcards, and T-shirts. There were pounds of Pirate's Booty salt-water taffy and solid chocolate alligators in a variety of sizes, including a two-pounder. And then we saw the thirteen-foot gator.

The length advertised on the billboards was no exaggeration. The gator was not in a pond or a tank; he was unrestrained. As we moved closer, we noticed he was not even alive. I told the kids, "Well, maybe, a taxidermist preserved him." Closer inspection revealed that the thirteen-foot gator, the pride of the Florida Citrus Center celebrated on signs every few miles on Florida's Interstate 10, is plastic.

We laughed out loud at the fake animal, took a picture, and left with a quart of Pirate's Booty salt-water taffy.

Our experience, at first, fell short of the wonder we imagined traveling along I-10. Domenic, Anna, and I have told the story of the Florida Citrus Center many times. A real gator with unlimited fruit samples would barely be remembered today. Instead, our I-10 journey with stops at no expectations, great expectations, disappointment, and then laughter has been shared with many. I am reminded that some of my favorite memories are times when things don't go as planned. Sometimes, time can transform disappointment into laughter. And when the laughter subsides, its residue leaves a wonderful memory.

The empty container of Pirate's Booty salt-water taffy sits on the kitchen counter like a trophy. It is plastic, just like the gator.

Thanks for all you do.

SEPTEMBER 2013

Let's be careful out there.

WITH those words, Sgt. Phil Esterhaus closed his daily *Hill Street Blues* roll call report at the beginning of each episode of the 1980s police drama. In the dark precinct station, Esterhaus told the officers and detectives assembled about the day's assignments and the latest perils in their unnamed city. He sent them off with "Let's be careful out there," and then the show's somber theme song began.

Be careful. Be safe. Why do we say this? Does it work? Will public safety personnel be less careful if we don't say this to them? Does telling my driving teenage sons to be safe keep them a little closer to the speed limit? Sergeant Esterhaus must have known that his scruffy Hill Street crew wouldn't slow down in their pursuit of the bad guys just because he told them to be careful. Will these words change behavior? It's hard to say.

Telling a friend or loved one to be careful is as much for the teller as it is for the listener. *Be careful* can be a quick prayer, a little gift of encouragement. Just through the hearing, we hope they will go through the day guarded by the human connection those words make.

Newtown. Nairobi. Navy Yard. Our world suffers

more and more from fits of inexplicable horror brought on by the lesser angels of our nature. We must live in it. We must carry out the work of public service.

Let's be careful out there.

Thanks for all you do.

OCTOBER 2013

It's my last day as a kid.

JOHN, our oldest, turned eighteen this month. On the morning of the day before his birthday, he said, "It's my last day as a kid." His nostalgia surprised me. I had in mind he'd be thinking of his new adult status and what it might mean for expanded freedom while he's still living at home.

My last day as a kid. Those words were with me all day. Toward the middle of the afternoon, I realized I had to get a whiffle ball and bat. On his last day as a kid, we have to play whiffle ball—one more time.

It took me three stores in North Stafford before I found a whiffle ball and bat. I wasn't interested in the aluminum bats and glistening white balls they use on the varsity field; I needed the neon-colored plastic tools on which he perfected his craft early in his baseball days. I rushed around the stores to get home in time before the early fall sunset. We wolfed down dinner, and the entire family went to the front yard with a two-inch diameter banana-yellow whiffle bat and four orange whiffle balls.

We started with Three Flies Up where the first kid to catch three pop flies wins. Then John said, "Dad, I want to do my Ten." It was mostly dusk by now. His siblings cleared the yard. His "Ten" is a game we started when he was little where I would hit ten pop flies and count how many he catches before the ball hits the ground. I start out with simply lofty pop flies, then short flies to make him run, and then long flies to make him stretch. Early in his little league days, it took him months to make Ten for Ten the first time. When we moved to Stafford, the Ten game became harder as we were playing whiffle ball on a steep yard. We haven't played it in years. On the day before his eighteenth birthday, he was Ten for Ten. And then, it was dark.

John thanked me for a fun night. After we finished playing, it occurred to me that maybe this wasn't so much about John's nostalgia as his dad's. On his last day as a kid, I was able to be a kid again too.

If you see me in the Government Center courtyard with a whiffle bat in hand, please come join me.

Thanks for all you do.

November 2013

Artwork by Nathan.

THAT'S what the plans said: "Artwork by Nathan." LeAnn Ennis, senior planner, was looking through archived development plans in the Old Chichester building. She came across a doodle her three-year-old son had done on work she brought home one night. After Nathan finished, LeAnn labeled the page "Artwork by Nathan." Nathan is now twenty-one, and his masterpiece has been carefully protected for eighteen years by the guard mice of the Old Chichester building.

Nathan's is one example of why local government is a family business. How many memos are stained by formula where a late-night feeding became time to catch up on work? And when the evening dishes are cleared, how many kitchen tables become home offices? While most of our citizens rest on holidays and snow days, for many of us, it's just another day on the job. And during every natural disaster, we leave our spouses to mind the house, shovel snow, or batten down the hatches for the coming hurricane. Our preparations for any impending emergency must include the home front because the sacrifice and burden of public service is borne as much by our families as us. As our friends in military service understand well, public service is a family business.

You might say Team Stafford is not just the 996 of us on payroll today but also our spouses and family, like Nathan eighteen years ago. Including husbands, wives, sons, daughters, mothers and fathers, Team Stafford is well over four thousand strong.

Nathan's artwork reminds us that we can't take care of Stafford without the people who take care of us. Local government is a family business.

In this season of gratitude, to all of Team Stafford—four thousand strong—thanks for all you do.

DECEMBER 2013

DIANE had a two-hug morning.

Domenic, sixteen, was headed to Stafford High School on the first day of *A Christmas Carol* in which he was performing. Excited about the show, he gave my wife, Diane, a hug, put his backpack together for the day, and then gave her another hug. The two successive hugs were such a marvel that she had to tell me about them.

With three teenagers in our house, hugs are rare commodities. Indeed, when a hug does come, I know it is time to change the batteries in our smoke alarms. The teenager hug is quick, from the side, and with little arm movement—as if they are pulling a hot slice of bread from the toaster while wearing a straitjacket. Thank goodness for the fist bump that provides a little connection without embarrassment when nonfamily members are watching.

When the kids were younger, hugs were frequent, and I took them for granted. They were tight and sloppy, sometimes followed by big wet cheek kisses. Selfishly, the best hugs were when they were hurt. Falling off their bike or walking into a wall, they would wrap their arms as far around me as they could and lay their head on my shoulder. Their dead, sobbing weight was as healing for me as the hug was for them. I remember when they were really little, I could spread my arms in front of me, and they'd come running. If they ran fast enough, the hug and sloppy wet kiss would knock me over. Now I know why people are so excited about grandchildren.

Wait a minute! I just figured it out. Teenagers are stingy with hugs so that we will appreciate those rare hugs all the more. Well, maybe if I keep telling myself that . . .

This Christmas, I hope your loved ones give you many two-hug mornings.

Thanks for all you do.

And May God bless us, every one.

February 2014

MILDRED Fogg was unhappy. Often. When I was town manager in West Point, Virginia, Mrs. Fogg would storm into town hall and demand to see "that damn town manager"! I never really understood exactly why she was angry. She was the kind who would be upset at the wind for making the leaves noisy. She expressed her angst with harsh words and pointed bent arthritic fingers topped with Coca-Cola red nail polish. I learned to listen quietly because responding would only fuel the fire. When she would finish her barking, I would say, *Nice to see you, Mrs. Fogg,* and my courtesy would only infuriate her more.

One day, I brought in a chocolate chess pie for everyone to share. This pie is a family recipe of butter, evaporated milk, sugar, and cocoa that makes a delicious, dense dessert. I was cutting a piece when I heard my name: *Where's that damn town manager?* She stormed up to me, and before she could say anything, I said *Here, Mrs. Fogg, have a slice of pie.* I don't know what came over me to do that. There was an awkward silence that seemed to last an hour. She looked me over, put her Coca-Cola red-tipped fingers back in their holsters, took the pie, and grunted *Humph.* She tasted it, and I invited her to sit down to eat. We had a conversation.

After the pie, when she came in to town hall, she would ask for "Anthony." As the fog of her angst lifted, complaints were replaced by stories about her younger years or her latest flower plantings.

While delicious, chocolate chess pie has no heart-changing powers. It was the simple act of giving her the pie — that human connection — that changed her heart toward me. And her acceptance of the pie changed my heart toward her.

A slice of chocolate chess pie changes two hearts - there are no small acts in public service.

Thanks for all you do.

APRIL 2014

SPRING brings warmer temperatures, new leaves and flowers, lots of rain, and best of all, baseball.

Baseball is a sport that doesn't inspire ambivalence. People either love the game or would rather light their hair on fire than watch it. Like it or not, baseball is full of life lessons, and here's nine innings of my favorites:

Win Some / Lose Some—A major league baseball season has 162 games. Every team will win sixty games and lose sixty games. What makes the difference is what they do with the other forty-two games.

Failure Is Abundant—Outstanding hitters will be out seven times in ten at bats. Hall of Fame pitchers will give up two or three earned runs in every game.

Greatness Comes with Continued Improvement—The difference between a .250 and a .300 hitter is only one hit per week (see *Random Thoughts* February 2013).

Practice Makes Excellence—What does every little leaguer, every girl's softball player, and every major leaguer do before a game? Play catch. Fundamentals must be practiced—all the time.

Effort Matters—If there's one thing that kids do
that hurts their game, it's not swinging through
the ball. Follow-through in a baseball swing is
critical, and many young players stop moving
as soon as they make contact, losing the power
inherent in their swing. How often have we
swung gently when the moment called for us to
swing so hard our body would spin with the bat?

Know Yourself—All batters can see at least three
pitches, if they allow themselves. Too often,
young hitters come out swinging at "junk"
instead of finding their pitch. A clever pitcher
may be smart enough not to give you your pitch,
so you'll have to wait him out for something to
hit. Find your pitch, and when it comes, swing
hard.

All Must Sacrifice—Even the best hitters have to hit
a sacrifice bunt or fly ball to help the team score
a run.

Stay Humble—Touchdowns, slam dunks, and
homeruns bring some of the worst displays
in sport. Pitching seems to be the last bastion
of sportsmanship. When a pitcher strikes out
a batter to end the inning, the pitcher walks
off the field with his eyes on his shoelaces.
Everyone in the stadium knows he bested the
batter, and it would be unseemly to humiliate a
fellow player.

There's No Place Like Home—Baseball is the only
major sport where the player, not the ball, scores
the run. No matter how well you play the game,
if you don't make it home, you don't score a
run. Good advice for all of us as we consider
what's most important to us.

The hot dogs are boiled. The foul lines and batter's
box are painted. Let's step up to the plate.

Thanks for all you do.

MAY 2014

MAY 27. Happy birthday, Stafford.

In the early 1660s, the population of Westmoreland County was burgeoning, so Virginia's governor ordered the creation of a new county to its west. On May 27, 1664, government began in Stafford with the first court proceeding.

A new place was born—in a new territory, in the new world—70 years before George Washington, more than a century before American independence, two centuries before the Civil War, 250 years before Quantico, and 300 years ahead of Interstate 95.

For me, 350 years is hard to fathom. Our County has had 127,837 days. Some 2.1 million people have lived here over the course of our history (my unscientific estimate). In 1664, America had 25 counties; today, we are among the 80,000 units of government in the United States. Descendants of Stafford's founders would be their great-great-great-great-great-great-great-great-great-great grandchildren (great[10]).

Stafford's story is told not only in the broad strokes of history but also in the daily living of its people. And each of us is a contributing author to that story as we provide ordinary services in a most extraordinary way.

Stafford's story—chapter 351—begins tomorrow. How fortunate are we to write history.

Thanks for all you do.

JUNE 2014

SOMETIMES, there is nothing like the real thing. I recently saw the original *Nighthawks* by Edward Hopper. Painted in 1942, *Nighthawks* is now an iconic image of an urban diner with a young waiter and three people sitting at the counter. I gave it passing glances in the books and websites where I've seen it dozens of times, and yet when I saw the original, I couldn't stop looking at it and saw details I'd never observed. With the painting created during World War II, Hopper keeps the image very dark outside of the restaurant (as if to mark an impending air raid drill) while the inside of the restaurant is bathed in yellow light. There is a couple at the counter, a man in a dark suit with his right hand on the counter and his left hand out of view on his lap. Sitting next to him is a red-haired woman in a red dress with unadorned hands. They drink coffee and appear to be tolerant of but uninterested in the waiter. Around the counter, a sinister dark-suited man with his back to the image sits alone. Both men have their hats on in the restaurant as if to suggest they are about to leave or just arrived. I soaked in the image for a long time, standing motionless except to move my eyes from one figure in the painting to the next. I left it only when I was dragged away.

I visited the enormous Yankee Candle story in

Williamsburg recently. As big as a Wal-Mart, they had
scents for every occasion, including food. The clerk
explained the proper method to smell a candle in a jar:
*Don't smell the wax on the top of the candle. To get the full effect,
smell the inside of the cap.* I was excited when I saw a Turkey
and Stuffing candle, and I put my nose deep inside to take
a full drag of the scent. It was weird and nothing like the
November smell of cooked Tom, with real turkey gravy,
and family and friends in our house.

A friend of mine recently lost his father. In his last
few days, his dad stopped eating, so my friend asked him
if there was anything he would like to have. His dad asked
for a Coke in a glass bottle. After a search, he found one
and brought it to his dad. Is there anything so good as
the sweet icy waterfall of Coke coming across thick glass?

E-mail, texting, Instagram, Twitter, Skype, and the
ten more communication tools that will be invented in the
next twelve months are gifts to our modern world. They
flatten our earth and connect us to souls whom we may
never meet in person. These are wonderful and comple-
mentary, but they're not the real things. Twenty-two years
in local government and I still like to see citizen concerns
with my own eyes. Pictures and descriptions often don't
do justice. What seems like a small thing in the office
becomes an epiphany in the field when I see the real thing.

In magazines, posters, and websites, I glanced at
Nighthawks. In person, I couldn't take my eyes off it. I
didn't know *Nighthawks* until its image marinated in my

head. How can we truly know someone until we look into his eyes and feel the space between a handshake?

Please pass the bottle opener.

Thanks for all you do.

JULY 2014

I just had the best haircut of my life.

My hair doesn't grow long. It grows big. When my hair was as big as I could stand, I went in for a haircut, and that's when I met Elizabeth.

In these dog days of summer, I wanted a cut short enough to stay cool but long enough so I don't look ready for Parris Island. I asked for a #3 on the side and a trim and thinning shears on the top. Elizabeth was particularly methodical with the #3 blade, so I asked her how long she had cut hair. Sixteen years, she said. She told me she started her work life as a nurse but cut hair all along also. The first of fifty grandchildren, Elizabeth was raised by her grandmother who wanted her to be a nurse.

She moved from the razor to the scissors and explained to me that she worked in nursing homes for a few years as a floor nurse, but it just wasn't her passion, so she turned to hair work full time. She switched to the thinning shears and told me she's considering going back to school for her BS in nursing but loves what she does with hair, so she's not sure.

Elizabeth brushed the hair off my neck and put a mirror behind my head, so I could confirm her handi-work. I told her she forgot to cut out the gray, a joke she must hear twenty times a week. She laughed as if she'd heard it for the first time and pulled the gray-hair-covered cape off my lap. I paid, thanked her, and headed out. Cutting hair is Elizabeth's calling. She serves many people in a job she loves. I've had countless forgettable haircuts in my life. This one I will not forget.

We have many Elizabeths here on Team Stafford. What a gift it is to work with people who love what they do and just can't hide it. To paraphrase Catherine of Siena: *if you do what you are meant to do, you will set the world on fire.*

Thanks for all you do.

AUGUST 2014

JOHN, our oldest, started college this week.

On move-in day, we waited in line behind all the SUVs and minivans, took our allotted time to unload, and fought the Wi-Fi in his room until it connected.

As we finished unpacking the car, a maudlin movie flashed through my head replaying John throughout the years. I remembered his first birthday when he whimpered all night with a stomachache because we let him eat as much cake as he could. I remembered him saying his first word "ball," our first trip to see the Yankees play, and his last swing on the Stafford High School ball field. I recalled when he cheated on a third-grade test, and I made him confess to his teacher. He had his revenge this past summer when he made me do cardio and weightlifting at the Y. I'm still sore.

The movie stopped as my brain scolded my heart: *Yes, he's leaving, but he's only ninety miles away, and he'll be home for Thanksgiving in a flash.*

When we returned home, I went to his room and found that he left us a teenager's present. A wet towel was on the bed, his laundry basket was full, and the bed sheets appeared to have been washed last during the George W. Bush presidency. I wasn't mad. The laundry was a good distraction.

There is no SAT for parenting, no college preparatory exam to ensure we are ready for this transition. This great gift in life comes as many do, in painful wrapping.

Saturday afternoon, we said our good-byes, and John walked away from us. I watched him go, and the movie started playing again. He wasn't a man walking away from his family to college; he was a little boy with new blue jeans and a backpack getting on the bus headed to his first day in kindergarten.

The movie stopped again. John stood at the curb and waited with another freshman to cross the street. He introduced himself, and they walked together. A new chapter begins.

Thanks for all you do.

September 2014

NAVY Hill was nowhere to be found.

As a newly hired intern in 1992 with a still-wet-ink college diploma, I was the "to whom it may concern" guy in the Richmond City Manager's Office. So when Bob Curry called for help with his Navy Hill Memorial, I was assigned the project.

A senior citizen, Mr. Curry wanted to recognize and remember the Navy Hill neighborhood. With more confidence than knowledge, I said, "Mr. Curry, I know our city very well, and I've never heard of Navy Hill. Are you sure that's what you mean?"

He sighed and explained, "Son, you've never heard of Navy Hill because Navy Hill is gone. The government took it to build I-95."

Navy Hill was settled by German immigrants beginning in 1810. By the turn of the twentieth century, it was a vibrant community of working class blacks. The downtown Richmond neighborhood stretched from Third to Thirteen Streets and adjoined its sister community Jackson Ward, known as the Harlem of the South. In its day, Navy Hill School was the only Richmond public school to employ black teachers. One of its graduates, Maggie Walker, became the first female bank president in America. When the Richmond-Petersburg Turnpike (today's I-95) was built in the 1950s, Navy Hill was destroyed.

The city-owned site we selected for Mr. Curry's monument was a triangular piece, about the size of a bedroom, at the end of Sixth Street (named Navy Hill Drive). With a minimal budget, all he and his friends could afford was a small tombstone. We placed it low to the ground among the weeds at Sixth and Duval Streets with the busy interstate at its back.

Feeling nostalgic a couple of years ago, I went to take a look at my first project and found the tombstone gone and a biotech research office building on the site. I called some of my contacts and learned the monument was in storage until construction of the biotech park was completed. Today, the monument sits in the midst of the Virginia Biotechnology Research Park on East Jackson Street beneath a state historical marker that tells a little of the Navy Hill story.

The tombstone reads, "Love and memories never die as days roll on and years pass by. Deep in our hearts memories are kept of the ones we loved and shall never forget."

While all its buildings are gone, Navy Hill lives.

Thanks for all you do.

OCTOBER 2014

WE can learn a lot from our children.

One day this summer, I was headed out to pick up a quick lunch. My wife's sister and mother were with us, so my task was to grab eight burgers, fries, and drinks and return quickly to the hungry crew. My daughter Mary came along with me, and when we pulled up to the drive-thru, she stopped me from ordering eight plain burgers and fries. She knew everyone's preferences from condiments to side items to drinks, so she placed the order. When the lunch was served, each of us had the meal we would have ordered ourselves.

My approach was one size fits all, but Mary knew we could do better. She took a few moments thinking about each family member and then told me what to order. Her empathy transformed a fast-food meal into a feast of appreciation.

Sympathy is feeling bad for your friend because his shoes hurt. Empathy is walking a day in his shoes to understand his perspective. That empathetic walk in another's shoes is great exercise and a critical skill in both good customer service and exercising leadership.

Sometimes, the one "in charge" needn't always "take charge." I was driving the car and paying the bill, but I was the person less qualified to order lunch.

I keep the receipt from that lunch on my bulletin board as a reminder. Surely my lunch would have filled their stomachs; Mary's lunch filled their souls.

Thanks for all you do.

NOVEMBER 2014

I spent last Thursday afternoon in the Stafford Hospital emergency room.

That morning, I was headed to a meeting in Fairfax County where I would deliver the thirty-seven blankets donated by county staff for Syrian refugees. On the way, a raging headache hit me. I stopped at a Sunoco and paid $2.15 for four Tylenol. The headache grew worse, and after an hour, I began to feel a tingling and pain in my right arm and leg. I left the meeting early and from I-95 Southbound called Chief Lockhart for some medical advice. He told me I needed to see a doctor. I thanked him and said I was headed home for a nap. When I made it home, I told my wife, Diane, my symptoms and the fire chief's advice, and before I knew it, I was in the passenger seat headed to Stafford Hospital.

In the ER, I answered the same questions dozens of times. *No, I haven't been to Africa in the last three weeks. I have no known allergies. The pain feels like a 6 on a scale of 1–10, and it increases every time you ask me about it.*

Concerned that I had the makings of a stroke, the efficient and compassionate ER staff carried out a CT scan, an EKG, blood work, and asked more questions. A cocktail including IV Benadryl was given, and we waited for test results.

During my ER visit, a baby was born at Stafford Hospital. I know this because "Twinkle Twinkle Little Star" played on the intercom. For a few seconds, everyone in the hospital shared in the celebration of this new little soul:

> Twinkle, twinkle little star,
> How I wonder what you are.
> Up above the world so high,
> Like a diamond in the sky.
> Twinkle, twinkle little star,
> How I wonder what you are.

About an hour passed, and Dr. Wright came in and told me that I had experienced a "complex migraine," which can cause pain in the leg and arm while the head pounds. So despite the symptoms, it was no stroke, she explained, just a middle-aged guy with a big headache.

Listening to "Twinkle Twinkle" in the ER reminded me of the countless blessings in my life. "Twinkle Twinkle" was the tune Diane sang to help our son Domenic fall asleep when he was a baby. I'm not sure if it was the nostalgia for Domenic's childhood, the thought of that new little soul upstairs in the hospital, or the IV cocktail, but soon after "Twinkle Twinkle" played, the pain of the headache went away.

When our blessings seem too many to count, that's when we must keep counting. Among these blessings for me is each of you. I am especially grateful to the many of you who will work this holiday week. While the rest of our county sits down to turkey, stuffing, and football, many of our Team Stafford colleagues will head to work. Like the good people of the Stafford Hospital ER, public service takes no holidays.

In that hospital bed, I vowed to count my blessings every time I hear "Twinkle Twinkle." To the men and women of Team Stafford—997 strong—I wish you and your families a happy Thanksgiving.

Thanks for all you do.

DECEMBER 2014

THIS *Random Thoughts* is PG-13; no young children allowed to read.

With seventeen years of service to our four kids, the Tooth Fairy has hung up her wings. After my daughter Anna had two teeth pulled, I went to sleep determined I could perform my Tooth Fairy responsibilities in the early morning. At about 5:30 a.m., as I was searching under her pillow for the tooth holder, she woke up. The jig was up. The Tooth Fairy myth ended.

A few days later, an earthquake of truth shook Anna's world when she connected her Tooth Fairy epiphany to Santa Claus and the Easter Bunny.

As young children, we have a sense of wonder and magic about Santa, the Easter Bunny, and the Tooth Fairy. When we learn the truth as older children, we are disappointed at first but then delight in keeping the world's best-kept secret from children younger than us (or revealing the secret to kids we didn't like). The best part comes, though, as adults when we become Santa, the Easter Bunny, and the Tooth Fairy.

Is there a Santa Claus? Is the Tooth Fairy real? And the Easter Bunny, does he exist? The world's best-kept secret is not that they don't exist; it's that they live on through adults who know "the truth."

Thanks for all you do. And may God bless us, every one.

FEBRUARY 2015

CRIKEY has a new home.

Crikey is a leopard gecko that spent the first year of his life in a converted fish tank. After a year's worth of mealworms and crickets caused Crikey to grow, my son Domenic determined his pet needed a larger place. PetSmart had a nice cage for $80.

Buying gas all fall semester without a job to replenish his bank account, Domenic was short on cash, so he hoped for gift cards for Christmas. They came. Over the holiday break, Domenic decided instead of buying the cage, he would build it himself. I was skeptical knowing that our home improvement abilities are limited, and it was unlikely that the entire project would cost less than $80.

Domenic was resolute. He hand drew a concept plan. Then he and my son John bought two by fours and wood screws at Lowe's. We dusted off the rarely used circular saw and a card table in the driveway became our sawhorse. The wood was measured once and cut twice for accuracy. Next, a slab of plywood was cut for the bottom of the cage. We drilled pilot holes and tried to place each screw flush with the wood. Most went in nicely; others went in less than straight. Once the shell was built, Domenic sanded all the wood. Hidden among twenty-plus cans of old paint in our garage, a small can of wood stain was just enough for our daughter Mary to give the cage a rich brown color.

Domenic measured the openings in the wood and headed to Lowe's for some cut glass. He pasted the glass to the wood frame. The grate from the old cage covered a portion of the top. The rest of the top was covered with a piece of plywood hinged to the side of the cage with an old door pull from our kitchen cabinets attached to it.

After the stain cured one night in the garage, Domenic placed his new creation in his room next to his bed and introduced Crikey to his new pad. A heat lamp sits on top of the metal grate to simulate Crikey's native habitat.

With imperfect corners and some screw heads bulging out of the wood, the homemade cage cost just over $60.

What is it about the things we make ourselves? Our own creations, our ideas, our tenacity, particularly in times when tenacity exceeds our talent, are reflections of who we are. Do we admire those around us for their strengths as much as we cherish them for who they are despite their human limitations? Like poorly set screws and inexact cut two by fours, the imperfections we have are what make us human.

Can a leopard gecko feel love? I don't know, but when he basks under that heat lamp in his new cage, I'm sure I see a smile on his face.

Thanks for all you do.

MARCH 2015

WHEN I told my kids this past December we were taking a day trip to the Library of Congress to see the *Magna Carta*, they were unhappy. *Not another historic trip, Dad. It's Christmas Break, and I learned enough during school. Can't you find another way to torture us? Wasn't the tour of President Buchanan's house enough?* I wouldn't relent. We had to see the "Great Charter."

There are four copies of the 1215 *Magna Carta* in existence, and one was on display in Washington, DC, for only a short time before it would be returned to England. On the drive north, I made my kids take off their headphones for a quick lesson.

King John of England signed the *Magna Carta* under duress when forty of his noblemen threatened to revolt. While the *Magna Carta* was written to protect the rights of aristocracy and not the common Englishman, it did introduce the rule of law, separation of powers, fair trial, and due process. Only ten weeks after its execution, the document was nullified.

And yet the *Magna Carta* lives. In 1297, it was reissued and is part of English law and its principles incorporated in the American Constitution. The *Magna Carta's* promise not to "sell or delay or deny justice" can be found on Stafford County's former seal. In 2008, writing for a majority of the US Supreme Court, Justice Anthony Kennedy cited the *Magna Carta* in a case related to an unlawful detainment.

My in-car lecture completed and my kids' eyes fully glazed over, we approached the Library of Congress, our first time there. The building itself is a monument, its grandeur worthy of the masterful works of human achievement in literature, science, history, and biography that line its shelves. We saw Thomas Jefferson's personal library collection and a Gutenberg bible.

Yellowed from the centuries but well preserved, the "Great Charter" is about twenty-four inches square and earns its name not from its size but from its precedent and contents. We had to wait in line to see it, and with others waiting behind us, we had only a few seconds to try to discern a few words in the scripted Latin.

I went through the line three times, and as I waited, I imagined myself at Runnymede watching the reluctant king sign the Great Charter to keep his kingdom intact. The daydream ended with my kids reminding me of my extreme nerdiness and that it was time for lunch.

Eight centuries ago, forty angry noblemen unwittingly planted a seed that helped grow the garden of American self-government. How blessed am I to cultivate that garden every day.

This spring break, we're headed to the National Archives. I can't wait to tell my kids.

Thanks for all you do.

APRIL 2015

THIS past Friday morning, I had a meeting with twenty-seven scientists.

Some of these scientists have Minecraft T-shirts, and others wear pigtails. Their laboratory is Room 208 at Grafton Village Elementary School under the supervision of Mrs. Roland, chief of research for the third grade. Our subject was surface tension. Living in a house with three teenagers and working in public service, I claimed to be an expert in surface tension. But our charge last Friday was not the metaphorical surface tension of daily life; it was real science.

Five desks were pushed together to make a table, and I squeezed into a little blue plastic chair next to my four fellow researchers. Our experiment was to use water from a medicine dropper and place it on a paper towel, copy paper, aluminum foil, and wax paper. Once the drop of water fell on the surface, we were tasked to observe the changes to the water and the surfaces on which it landed. Each table had a "materials manager" responsible for handling the supplies and a "reporter" to share the collected observations of each group.

Mrs. Roland gave us instructions on how to use the medicine dropper. I was reminded by the children's marveling that the medicine dropper is a fascinating device. *Squeeze the top and water comes in? Squeeze it again and water goes out? How does that work? It works with no batteries or Wi-Fi!*

The first three tests were with the copy paper, the paper towel, and the foil. The kids were interested but not surprised by what happened with the water and these surfaces. They were astounded, however, at the results from the wax paper. A drop of water remained intact on the wax paper, and with the tip of the medicine dropper, you could move the water droplet around the wax paper and leave no moisture in its path. We all agreed that was really cool. In fact, if I had learned about water and wax paper at Bon Air Elementary School in the 1970s, I have long since forgotten.

Like they were defending new science in front of the Nobel committee, each reporter presented the experimentation of his or her group. We applauded them, and the scientists headed to lunch. The sign on the wall said it was cheeseburger day at the Grizzlies' cafeteria, and I was hoping for a lunch invitation, but the scientists eat alone. Disappointed, I was consoled when three scientists gave me a farewell hug and two complimented my choice of necktie.

The beaded water on the wax paper flooded my brain with a river of memories from school. How I love to learn and to wonder. When my daydream ended, I thought how infrequently we say, "I never knew that before." It takes courage as an adult to admit ignorance and to show wonder. Sometimes, it's hard enough to face up to what we know we've learned and forgotten. What our world could be if adults were measured not so much by what we know but by how much we wonder and imagine.

The scientists of the Grafton Village Elementary School Room 208 Laboratory are at work again today. I wonder what they'll discover.

Thanks for all you do.

MAY 2015

THE basketball disappeared.

Anna hopes to play for the Drew Middle School basketball team next year in the seventh grade. Practicing her craft one night in the driveway, the ball bounced off the backboard, rolled down the driveway across the neighbor's yard, into the ditch, and then turned left and followed the ditch into the culvert pipe under our driveway. The diameter of the pipe is barely greater than the ball, so this "nothing but net" entrance into the culvert was quite a feat. Why couldn't all our shots be that good?

With dusk approaching and rain in the forecast, the mission for Anna and me was clear—get the ball out tonight. Our task seemed impossible when I remembered my sixteen-foot tree pruner was on loan to a friend, and my across-the-street neighbor who has every tool known to man wasn't home.

We separated two broom handles from their brushes and lashed them together with duct tape. Anna crouched down on one end of the pipe, and I pushed the broom handles in on the other. She saw the ball move but just barely. We needed more length. I found two walking sticks from our boys' scouting days. The four handles were connected with more duct tape. We took our same positions. I pushed while Anna looked. She said, "I see

181

leaves moving but no ball, Dad." Dusk grew darker, so Anna held a flashlight into the pipe to see. I found an old two by four, and two more rakes were stripped of their handles making a seven-piece basketball rescue pole. Anna resumed the position and noticed that "the leaves are moving. Keep pushing, Dad." I kept pushing, but nothing seemed to budge.

Almost night now, I yelled to Anna, "Stick in your hand and see if you feel anything!" She did and it was the ball. It made it to our side of the driveway in the culvert. But we couldn't pull it out. Years of accumulation of dirt blocked the other end of the pipe leaving a hole smaller than the ball. I dug in the dark with Anna holding the flashlight, and finally, the ball was freed. We hosed off the ball (and ourselves) and placed a brick at the culvert opening on my neighbor's side to ensure no ball would find its way in there again.

It wasn't pretty, and to those driving by, we must have looked strange lying prostrate in the ditch shoving sticks tied by duct tape into a driveway pipe. But our mission was accomplished.

Sometimes in public service, we have all the people, equipment, and time we need to get the job done. More often, our assignments exceed the time and resources we have. How do we close the gap? Hustle. Hustle is that purposeful effort that goes above and beyond to get the job done. That's Team Stafford. Hustle is part of our DNA, and while others may have more people and money, nobody outhustles Team Stafford.

The rake and broom handles have all been restored to their mates. While we still have plenty of duct tape, I'm glad it's softball season.

Thanks for all you do.

June 2015

Just gotta embrace it.

THAT was a text from my older brother when I told him that with my recent forty-fifth birthday, I couldn't deny middle age.

If age is a state of mind, I'm not sure I want to visit the state of middle age. My hair is more gray than black. Two of my children are adults. Too many of my sentences begin with "did I tell you this before?"

The good news is that I'm still younger than the president, and my waistline is now firmly below my age.

I've asked my kids' friends to start calling me Big Tony since hearing Mr. Romanello over and over really makes me feel old. Big Tony wears shorts and untucked T-shirts on the weekends, sometimes doesn't shave, and certainly can't be anywhere near middle-aged.

Maybe I'm taking all this middle-age anxiety too seriously. I should remember leadership guru Ben Zander's rule #6: "Don't take yourself too seriously." What are Zander's rules 1–5? you ask. There aren't any.

Remember rule #6 . . . Did I tell you this before?

Thanks for all you do.

About the Author

ANTHONY Romanello has made his career serving local governments in Virginia. He worked for the City of Richmond in various roles from 1992 to 2000 including four years as assistant to the city manager. He was town manager of West Point from 2000 to 2003. From 2003 to 2007, he was deputy county administrator for Stafford County, Virginia. On January 1, 2008, he became Stafford's sixth county administrator.

Anthony has a bachelor of arts in history and American government with a minor in religious studies from the University of Virginia and a master of public administration from Virginia Commonwealth University. He is a credentialed manager through the International City/County Management Association (ICMA).

Anthony is a graduate of the Harvard Kennedy School's Senior Executives in State and Local Government program and the University of Virginia's Senior Executive Institute. He is an adjunct faculty member in the George Mason University and Virginia Tech Master of Public Administration programs.

Anthony is an Eagle Scout and, in 2015, was recognized by the National Eagle Scout Association as an Outstanding Eagle Scout.

Anthony and his wife, Diane, live in Falmouth, Virginia, with their four children.